FINAL DEPARTURE

A STEP-BY-STEP-GUIDE TO PREPARE FOR ONE'S PASSING

ANDREA COX

TESTIMONIALS

Andrea is an exceptional Pre-Planning Consultant. She not only listened and answered all my questions, but also thoroughly explained all my options in detail. She ensured that I understood everything which made me very comfortable with all the choices made.

I really appreciated her professionalism and would highly recommend her services.

V Watt
Calgary, AB

At the beginning of 2021, I had this urge to ensure I put my affairs in order to secure my final resting place, until Jesus comes. My first thought was to call Andrea Cox as I had attended one of her seminars. That was one of the best decisions of my life. Andrea's vast knowledge of the subject matter, calm approach, engaging personality and professional approach made me quite comfortable.

She did the heavy lifting by researching funeral homes and cemeteries in my area and provided sound recommendations. It was easy for me to make an informed decision and Andrea took care of the necessary paperwork.

The process was stress free and my loved ones are spared the additional pain of having to make arrangements after my passing.

Sharon Long, BA, BSW, RSW
Edmonton, AB

As I planned grandma's funeral, Andrea Cox was there to help me every step of the way, her knowledge of what needed to be done was very evident.

She used her loving, calm, and gentle personality to guide me through a difficult time with ease. Andrea was happy to know that grandma had her funeral prearrangement set up, making it easier to carry out her final wishes.

In the end because of Andrea's commitment, care and help we had peace of mind.

Tecla C
Calgary, AB

We have worked with Andrea Cox for two funeral events and on both occasions, we've had great experiences. Andrea was knowledgeable, resourceful, and kind--especially as she took the time to understand the proper funeral etiquette specific to our family's culture and spiritual practises.

Andrea helped us plan our funerals in advance so our family and friends won't have to carry the burden of making funeral arrangements during their time of grief.

We were so pleased with Andrea's professional pre-planning services, it made sense to rehire her to plan and execute our late brother's Celebration of Life Ceremony.

Andrea is your person from creating a program, to organising tasks, to hosting a funeral, to just offering a comforting hug, and everything in between. Andrea took care of it all with ease and class, which put my family's mind at peace. It was such a joy to know with certainty that we didn't need to worry, because everything had been taken care of.

Michelle J Buckle
Toronto, ON

A couple of years ago my wife and I went to a seminar with Andrea as the spokeswoman. After the seminar, we met with Andrea and she was amazing and helped us with all of our wishes for the final journey.

Jim and Evelyn Wolden
Kelowna, BC

I had the pleasure of working with Andrea when a loved one passed and we didn't have the support of his family to mitigate the funeral arrangements. Andrea helped to keep me calm and was able to explain the intricate workings of the funeral home and various government associations.

I appreciated her coaching as at the time I didn't have a lot of resources at my disposal. I wouldn't hesitate to recommend her for when you have questions or need additional support.

Jerilyn Wolstenholme, BBA
Calgary, AB

I was referred to Andrea through a close friend and it is the best thing that could have happened. Death is a conversation that I did not like to talk about, but talking to Andrea about it with another close friend made me feel comfortable. We found Andrea easy to talk to, knowledgeable, and very helpful. She walked us through the process of putting a plan in place which made it easy for us to start the process of getting our funeral pre-arrangements set up.

Not leaving a burden on my family especially after losing our brother made my decision even easier because of our experience. Running around trying to put things in place for our brother while in distress was devastating and not easy. Especially because his passing was sudden and my siblings and I were not familiar with the process.

I would suggest anyone who has the opportunity before a death to take the time and speak with their family about their final wishes and put their final arrangements in place. Especially those who have health issues that are threatening, this would give them peace of mind knowing that the burden on their family while they are grieving will be taken away.

Setting up funeral arrangements and putting a plan in place is a gift of love to your family and brings peace of mind with ease when it is all done especially knowing that financially, it could be all taken care of.

Angella G
Edmonton, AB

Copyright © 2022 Andrea Cox

All rights reserved. No part of this book may be reproduced by any mechanical, photographic, or electronic process or in the form of phonographic recording; nor may it be stored in a retrieval system, transmitted, or otherwise copied for public or private use without the prior written permission of the author.

Andrea Cox
Licensed Pre-Planning Specialist
E-mail: admin@preplanfirst.com
Website: www.preplanfirst.com

ISBN 978-1-7779924-0-8 (Paperback)
ISBN 978-1-7779924-2-2 (Hardcover)
ISBN 978-1-7779924-1-5 (eBook)
ISBN 978-1-7779924-3-9 (IS Paperback)

Edited by Lori McCrae
Interior Layout and Design by Angelo Sainz Digital Creative Design
Cover design by Publish and Promote
Cover artwork by Angelo Sainz Digital Creative Design

Every reasonable effort has been made to trace ownership of copyright materials. Information enabling the author to rectify any reference or credit in future printings will be welcomed.

The information in this book is not intended as a substitute for medical, legal, financial, tax or other professional advice. It is strictly the opinion of the author based on the author's experience as a licensed funeral pre-planning consultant. It is recommended that you consult your applicable professional if you have concerns in these areas.

Printed and bound in Canada

DEDICATION

This book is dedicated to all End-of-Life Professionals who have helped families during the passing of a loved one, we see you and appreciate your work.

A special call out to all Unique End-of-Life Professionals who work tirelessly to encourage people to normalize talking about death and educate families and communities on the importance of pre-planning before the passing of a loved one.

This is not an easy career but do not give up. Find a partner with other Unique End of Life Professionals who can support and encourage you.

Continue to plant those seeds and one day, they are guaranteed to grow.

TABLE OF CONTENTS

Introduction 1

Chapter 1 - Welcome Aboard Flight 534229 (Legacy) 3
    1:1 – Six Steps to Preparing for your Final Departure 10

Chapter 2 - Celebration of Life 13
    2.1 – Celebration of Life During a Pandemic 18

Chapter 3 - Having the Conversation 21
    3:1 – Do Not Resuscitate Order (DNR) 25
    3:2 – Starting the Conversation 27

Chapter 4 - Final Wishes for Disposition 31
    4:1 – Cremation 35
    4:2 – Burial 38
    4:3 – Memorialization 40

Chapter 5 - Wills and Living Wills 43
    5:1 – What is a Will? 45
    5:2 – Who is an Executor (Personal Representative)? 47
    5:3 – Executor (Personal Representative) Ideal Characteristics 49
    5:4 – Executor (Personal Representative) Responsibilities 51
    5:5 – Bank Account 58
    5:6 – Common – Law Spouse 59
    5:7 – Holograph Wills 62
    5:8 – Living Wills 66

Chapter 6 - Insurance 69
    6:1 – Term Insurance Policy 72
    6:2 – Whole Life Policy 74
    6:3 – Universal Life Policy 75

  6:4 – Pre-Need Insurance Policy (Funeral Home Prepaid Policy)............77

  6:5 – Worldwide Travel Protection Policy....................................79

  6:6 – Accidental Death and Dismemberment Policy 81

Chapter 7 - Organ and Tissue Donation vs Body Donation 85

  7:1 – Organ and Tissue Donation..87

  7:2 – Body Donation for Medical Education................................. 89

Chapter 8 - Senior Care 93

  8:1 – Family Caregivers Filing System..95

  8:2 – Homecare Options for Seniors..97

Chapter 9 - Digital Legacy 99

  9:1 – Facebook Legacy Contact.. 103

Chapter 10 - Updating Documents on a Regular Basis 105

  10:1 – Significant Milestones to Update Documents........................ 108

Chapter 11 - Taxes 111

Chapter 12 - Prepaid Funeral Home and Cemetery Packages 115

  12:1 – Benefits of Prepaid Pre-Arrangements................................ 117

  12:2 – Payment Options... 119

  12:3 – Cremation Guaranteed 121

  12:4 – Low-Cost Repatriation Benefit... 124

Chapter 13 - Funeral Homes and Cemeteries 127

  13:1 – Funeral Homes.. 129

  13:2 – Cemeteries...132

Chapter 14 - End-of-Life Doula and Death Café 137

  14:1 – Death Café...139

  14:2 – End-of-Life Doula (Death Doula)..................................... 140

Chapter 15 - Grief 143

  15:1 – Ways to Alleviate Stress Before a Passing 145

15:2 – Grief Support 147

Chapter 16 - Bucket List and Creating Memories 149

Chapter 17 - Pictures/Obituary/Eulogy/Record a Song/
Letter Writing 153

17:1 – Pictures 155
17:2 – Obituary 157
17:3 – Eulogy 158
17:4 – Record a Song 160
17:5 – Letter Writing/Recording 161

Chapter 18 - Legacy 163

18:1 – Examples of Legacy 167

Chapter 19 - What to do with My Stuff 171

Chapter 20 - Challenge 175

Closing 177

In Memory of Folasade (Sade) Abiola 181

Letter of Instructions to My Loved Ones 185

What to Do at the Time of Death 187

When a Death Occurs 187
1-4 Hours After 189
4-12 Hours After 191
12-24 Hours After 192

Workbook 197

Certificate of Love 198
6 Steps to Preparing for Your Final Departure 199
Organ Donation or Body Used for Science 200
Funeral Home & Cemetery Contact Details 201

    Emergency Contact Details 203

    Family & Friends Contact Details 204

    Religious Leader/s Contact Details 212

    Important Documents Log 214

    Hardware Login Information 225

    Vital Statistics 227

    Funeral Home & Cemetery Instructions 229

    About Me (Obituary & Eulogy Information) 233

    Celebration of Life Instructions 241

    Letters for My Loved Ones 248

    My Legacy 253

    My Bucket List 255

    What To Do with My Stuff 259

    Notes 262

Grief and Bereavement Books 267

    Children Books 267

    Adult Books 268

Senior Care Books 269

Death Preparation Books 269

Family Game. 270

Meal Train 270

Things to Say to a Dying Person 271

What to Say and What Not to Say to a Griever 273

About the Author 276

Bibliography 277

Sponsors 278

FOREWORD

Seven years ago, Andrea, a local Canadian, born and raised in Calgary, Alberta, changed her career from a Staffing Consultant to helping families understand the importance of getting their affairs in order before they pass away.

In her work, she encountered too many unwilling to face the reality of what their death will mean to their family beyond the pain of the loss of not having them around. Andrea decided that she had to find a way to let everyone know what her experience has taught her, that ignoring the issue does not make it go away.

Andrea's book fills a need as many do not know what they should do to prepare for death or if they need to do anything until it is too late. She clears up misconceptions and takes away the taboo of the subject of death.

As you turn the pages of this book, Andrea's vast knowledge and experience are evident. She has done us a great service by tackling a delicate subject that invokes apprehension in many of us. Using the practical and relatable analogy of a journey by flight throughout the book shows the reader that life is a journey.

Just like a flight, no matter how long you fly, you get to the end of your destination where you must disembark, and for humans, the destination for life's journey as we know it is the end of our life, death.

A plane cannot fly forever, and humans do not live forever, at least, not yet anyway.

So, the big question to you, the reader, is, how will your death impact your loved ones? How will the death of your loved one impact you? To make it personal, aside from the grief your loved ones will undoubtedly feel on your passing, will you have left a mess behind? Will chaos, confusion, family disruption, unexpected financial obligations, and much more ensue after your death? Andrea is enlightening us that this is very likely if we do not plan.

As an Attorney who deals with Wills and Estate, I have witnessed first-hand the heartaches of families who lost a loved one without a Will; it is grief compounded by confusion, disharmony, infighting, anger, and so on.

However, the peace that follows when a person dies but has left their affairs in order brings comfort and peace amidst the grief that is quite simply immeasurable. The importance of a Will, Living Wills, cannot be overemphasized.

However, this book gives us more than that. It tackles the painful and delicate subjects of care for the dying. Have you heard of a death café and death doula? Do you know about all your choices regarding life insurance, funeral cost insurance, etc.? Have you thought about the kind of funeral service you would like to have, or if none at all? Do you know the implications of having your body or organs donated and the likely impact of the logistics on your family? What will happen if you die abroad? If your wish is to transfer your body to your original home country for those with foreign roots, how will this be done? Is your family aware of your wishes and choices in these matters?

Who will be the beneficiary of any benefit that arises from your death? Is it your current spouse, ex, children, stepchildren, etc.? Is your paperwork up to date? How about all the digital access that for the present only you know? Will your loved ones be able to access them?

Have you thought about the legacy you wish to leave behind and how you can start working on that legacy now?

This is a simple step-by-step guideline and workbook on what is needed on your journey to tackle these crucial matters and more. It is almost impossible not to understand every stage as she lays them out with simplicity and clarity.

So, join Andrea as she helps us prepare for our final departure in this tastefully and candidly written book. I challenge you not to learn something new. I learned many. Regardless of your age or the simplicity or complexity of your family and financial situation, you will likely benefit.

I urge you to reflect on this thought-provoking book, take the necessary actions, and keep it as a consultation guide. Inform others about it, share it with friends and family members, send it as a gift; why not. In my opinion, every household needs this book. Let's get comfortable talking about the journey to our final destination; let's be prepared; it's an act of love.

I thank my friend, Andrea Cox, for caring so deeply, and for sharing her unique insights with us. We are certainly better for it.

Charles Osuji
CEO, Osuji & Smith Lawyers

ACKNOWLEDGEMENTS

First, I want to thank God for choosing me to work in this Unique Career. If anyone had told me years back that I would be working in the Death and Dying Industry, I would not have believed them. It has been quite the journey.

A very special thank you to my parents, Calcen and Joyce Cox, my sister Natalie Senoo and her husband, Raymond Senoo; my twin brother Andrew Cox, nieces, and nephews - Akesha, Brayden, Nevaeh, Ashan and RayJ, other family, and friends, including my church family mainly at Bridgeland Seventh-day Adventist Church who have been patient with me while I figured out my God-given purpose. In the course of figuring out myself and what brings me the most peace, I did end up sacrificing much quality time. I do promise that going forward, that will change for the better as long as I am on this side of the earth.

Another special thank you to everyone who has been a part of my journey to self-publishing this book, especially the many hands that helped put it all together. This includes my Graphic Designer, John Sainz (Angelo Sainz) who designed the suitcase and did the interior of the book, I would not have been able to do this without you. Lori McCrae my Editor, Dawn James who offers various author services and created the idea with the spotlight on the cover of the book. Charles Osuji who wrote the forward and all the Professionals who either read a section or four before it went to the Editor ensuring I was not mixing up information…lol, this is Michael Pierson, Angela Yee-Hamshaw, Glen Griffiths, Mercy Maviko, Lorrie Morrales, Christine Brunsden, Anna Adams, Brian Dunn, and Marcy Norman. Also, all those who encouraged me and read through the book before it went to publishing, Wani Alali, Donnovan Simon, Chevonnie Walters, Juliette Omonigho, and Craig Learmont. Also, a very special thank you to all the Sponsors at the back of the book.

Last, but not least, a very, very special thank you to Bert Oberembt with Getting Your Affairs In Order who supported me in every way possible following my 2nd career change in this Industry and believing in my full potential. Also, Michael Pierson and David Root, with Pierson's Funeral Services, who took me under their wings and gave me a chance to train and work with their amazing staff. Pierson holds my Pre-Need Sales Licence through the Alberta Funeral Services Regulatory Board (AFSRB).

VII

INTRODUCTION

Welcome to Flight 534229 (Legacy), where we will be performing a practice run for our final departure. I hope you did not forget to pack your bucket list along with other essentials to prepare for this flight. Whether you are prepared for your final departure or not will affect your loved ones' experience. Yes, it will either be a smooth flight or a very turbulent one. But I do promise that if you pack most of the essentials that are recommended in this book, the flight will be smoother, especially for your loved ones.

In preparation for this flight, I will ensure that you are equipped, and your luggage is packed with the essentials needed to make this a memorable flight. No need to worry, I will ensure that we review all the safety features in detail with you. I strongly recommend that you refer to the local professionals in your area to ensure that you have the accurate information that is applicable to the country of your departure. Please note that the overall itinerary for your flight will vary based on the rules and regulations that are applicable to your city, province/state, and country.

Your final departure is a flight that we all must travel on, in other words, it is unavoidable. The importance of having a plan, or in this instance, a travel itinerary in place in the event you do not live to 120 years, is that it is the oxygen mask that you would leave for your loved ones if you do not make it.

Yes, we often do not want to think or talk about death; however, the more we talk about it and prepare our loved ones for the unavoidable, the result is a better way of handling one's passing. A final departure without a plan in place, in some cases, leaves chaos, confusion, family disputes, financial hardships, inability to properly grieve, involvement of external parties, such as the government, and most importantly, not having your final wishes being executed to your specifications.

The question is: What would it look like if you or another family member did not wake up tomorrow morning? The goal for this practice flight is to suggest possible answers to this question and help you and your loved ones to prepare for your final departure called – "death". Putting a plan in place today will bring peace of mind to your loved ones in the future.

Refer to Workbook Page(s):
Certificate of Love
Page: 198

Chapter 1

Welcome Aboard Flight 534229 (Legacy)

"Ladies and gentlemen, the Captain has turned on the Fasten Seat Belt sign. If you haven't already done so, please stow your carry-on luggage underneath the seat in front of you or in an overhead bin. Please take your seat and fasten your seat belt. Also make sure your seat back and folding trays are in the full upright position."

"A man who has not prepared his children for his own death has failed as a father." - *"Black Panther"*

Do you remember those words in the movie *"Black Panther"* that was released in 2018? It was the scene where the son told his father that he was not ready for him to die, and the father reminded him that he has been preparing him all his life to become King after he dies.

In reality, how many of us have been prepared for death or even know how to prepare for death? When I think about it, death is a part of life that is unavoidable and can be as beautiful as a birth once we fully accept and embrace it. But why is death treated like a taboo subject and why is talking about it often avoided? For years, I have wondered how society, communities and parents got it all wrong on the subject of death and how can I change this.

When a person dies, there is a likelihood of some things happening: chaos, confusion, family breakdowns, financial hardship and the list goes on.

What can we do to change that or alleviate the negative domino effect at the very least?

In the context of parenting, and when we think back to the movie *"Black Panther"*, they were implying that the point of parenting for both the father and the mother isn't about shielding our children from challenges and difficulty, but to prepare them for it.

As difficult as it is and as much as we do not want to discuss the topic of death, the truth is that we must do so before a crisis or a death occurs.

We can choose our difficulty level in terms of when we want to discuss death.

Here are a few options:

- Now, on a normal day
- During a crisis (e.g., a terminal illness)
- Or at the time of death

Choose your difficulty level.

Based on personal experience, if the discussion was not had and a terminal illness occurs, there is the possibility of that discussion becoming non-existent, in other words, it won't happen. Having this difficult conversation in a crisis typically results in a number of scenarios:

- The terminally ill person may not want to talk about it because they are already struggling with the reality and possible outcome of their illness.

- The loved ones are going through denial and would rather not talk about it.

- A loved one wants to talk about it, but they do not know how to bring it up.

Unfortunately, the devastating aspect of not having discussions about this unavoidable life occurrence, results in your loved ones having to decipher your final wishes whilst grieving. Is it fair that loved ones are left to put the pieces together in the midst of their grief? The option here is to choose your difficulty level, will it be before a crisis or at the time of death?

How early should we start talking to our children about death?

In my family, I find that my mother is scared of discussing death and I could not imagine her speaking to us about it at a younger age. In fact, death was not discussed much in our home growing up. If it did come up, it was because a family member or close family friend passed away.

I know many homes where death is a secret or continues to be a taboo topic. So where does this leave us? How do we break this taboo topic to be discussed in our homes?

When is the right time to speak about this taboo subject? Or should this be taught in the schools? And if taught in schools, at what age?

There is a large amount of resources on how to talk to children about death, but not what is a good age to start having the conversation.

Let's brainstorm the consequences of not having this crucial yet essential discussion about preparing for ones passing:

1. Unexpected surprises (not knowing what to expect).

2. Family breakdowns.

3. Financial hardship.

4. Experiencing the chaos of not knowing what to do when a death occurs.

5. Not knowing what funeral home to call, if using one.

6. Not having the money to cover the funeral expenses (i.e.: Funeral home and/or cemetery bill).

7. Spending more money at a funeral home because of a lack of advance research into available options.

8. Making permanent decisions that one might regret at a later date.

9. Not having a Will in place to provide guidance to your loved ones.

10. The challenging and lengthy process of overseeing an Estate when there is no Will.

11. Funds being disbursed from the Estate to individuals that were not a part of the deceased's life, or the deceased wouldn't approve of, for e.g.: ex-spouses

(due to incomplete legal divorce or not updating legal documents), estranged child/ren.

12. Traumatic experience for the person who is dying and the family.

13. Family's attempt to acquire a Will at the last minute before a passing occurs when they could be spending time with their dying loved one.

14. Depression.

15. Compounded Grief. Death is one thing but having to deal with a loved one's affairs because it was not done in advance adds to the grief.

This list can get extensive so instead of continuing down this negative list, let's take this to the next step. This book attempts to solve the following problems:

- Organizing and getting your affairs in order by following a step-by-step process.

- How to have the difficult conversation with your loved ones to normalize the discussion of death.

- Dealing with the diagnosis of a terminal illness, you can instead spend your last days with your loved ones and doing what you want to do with a peace of mind because a plan is in place.

- Ensuring that when you are no longer around, your loved ones will have a step-by-step guide on what to do when they need you the most.

- Leave a positive legacy.

Do you remember the days when the saying was "Here today, gone tomorrow"?

My mentor, Rhonda Green, recently said "Here one minute, gone the next."

Let's start having the conversation and putting a plan in place today so we can live life to the fullest with our families.

Chapter 1:1

Six Steps to Preparing for Your Final Departure

"Flight attendants/Cabin Crew, please prepare for gate departure."

"Flight attendants/Cabin Crew, doors on automatic, cross-check and report. Thank you."

"Ladies and gentlemen, I'd like to direct your attention to the television monitors. We will be showing our safety demonstration and would like the next few minutes of your complete attention."

"Now we request your full attention as the flight attendants demonstrate the safety features of this aircraft."

Step 1 - Have the Conversation with Your Family

- Senior care options
- Do Not Resuscitate (DNR)
- Organ(s) donation
- Final disposition wishes
- Where to find important documents
- What to do with your stuff (Property and belongings)

Step 2 - Get a Will and Two Living Wills

- Will
- Two Living Wills

Step 3 - Get Insurance

- Term Insurance
- Final Expense Insurance (i.e.:funeral home prepaid policy)

Step 4 - Research and Choose a Funeral Home and/or Cemetery

- Funeral Home
- Cemetery

Step 5 - Continue Completing Workbook

Step 6 - Live Life to the Fullest

Welcome again to Flight 534229 (Legacy), so you can understand the importance of getting your affairs in order.

Refer to Workbook Page(s): 6 Steps to Preparing for Your Final Departure Page: 199

Chapter 2

Celebration of Life

"Ladies and gentlemen, the Captain has turned off the Fasten Seat Belt sign, and you may now move around the cabin. However, we always recommend keeping your seat belt fastened while you are seated.

In a few moments, the flight attendants will be passing through the cabin to offer you hot or cold drinks, as well as breakfast/ dinner/supper/ (a light meal/a snack). Alcoholic drinks are also available at a nominal charge--with our compliments. (On long flights with inflight entertainment, we will be showing you our video presentation). Now, sit back, relax, and enjoy the flight. Thank you."

How do you want your family to celebrate you when you pass away?

Did you know that your final celebration is for your loved ones, not you?

Do you know the current restrictions for Celebration of Life gatherings in your area?

Celebration of Life is to give loved ones an opportunity to celebrate, honor and remember their loved one at the time of death. Not only that, but it also gives family and friends the opportunity to support each other as they cry, laugh, and take the time to grieve their loss. Celebration of Life gathering also starts the grieving process, especially when the death is sudden and there is an opportunity to say bye (especially if there is a viewing of the body).

How big or small can you envision your Celebration of Life to be?

Have you ever planned a wedding? How long did it take? 3 months, 6 months, 9 months, or a year? Celebrating one's life is the same level as birth, birthday, graduation, wedding, anniversary, etc. Depending on culture, beliefs, customs, etc., a Celebration of Life can end up being one of the biggest celebrations.

Do you have a preference for: colors, your favorite photographer? DJ or comedian, a crying station for people to cry at? (I heard the owner of New Narratives, Christina Andreola come up with this idea) alcohol, dancers, singers, - the list is endless.

Unfortunately, in some cases the death happens so quickly that trying to put something together is exceedingly difficult for those who are left behind. At times nothing is done at all and a Celebration is left to be planned for a potential future date. There can be several decisions that need to be made on a short notice regarding planning a "Celebration of Life" after a loved one passes away, and the family goes to the funeral home. Trying to put something together in the midst of grief can be mentally and emotionally impossible for some.

If we can see death as another milestone in one's life and a reason to celebrate amongst all the shock and grief, how much would that help those who are left behind? Yes, the pain and grief will still be there but having an amazing send-off and taking the time as family and friends to commemorate this celebration would be helpful and be much easier for those left behind to cope with mentally and emotionally.

Don't get me wrong, it is much, much harder when it comes to babies or children, and in all honesty, I cannot imagine that type of loss, but trying to find a reason to celebrate and honour that precious gem might still help in the long run.

My experience as a Licensed Funeral and Memorial Preplanner currently in Alberta and British Columbia has been a huge eye-opener. With my clients there's been an extreme difference between direct cremation (meaning no service or Celebration of Life) to a Full-Service Celebration of Life with a Burial. It came to the point that when I wrote up contracts for Direct Cremations, I asked the client's permission to write on their paperwork that their family can do what they like and what they need to help them through the loose. But taking note the direct cremation option has been paid for.

The reason why I decided to start doing this is because the more that I spoke with family members who did not have any service or Celebration of Life for their loved ones, the feedback I was getting was that they felt stuck in their grief and needed something to help them because they did not get the chance to either say their final goodbyes or take the time to memorialize this event of their loved one's life.

At times, making the decision on behalf of our family that we do not want them to do anything but to cremate us with no Celebration of Life gathering when we die is only helping them to be stuck and confused and might put them in a worse situation in the long run in their grief journey.

Overall, what does your Celebration of Life look like? Please keep in mind that it does not have to be expensive or extravagant. If birthdays, graduations, weddings, or anniversaries were never a big thing for your family then doing something small is just as sufficient. It could be as simple as having a Virtual Zoom Gathering with family and friends wearing your favourite colour and drinking your favourite drink. One may ask, what is a Virtual Zoom Gathering? It is a live gathering conducted over the Internet using web conferencing software and audio/video equipment. Zoom is an easy app to download on your phone or computer and is used by many since Covid both professionally and personally.

If the complete opposite is true for your family and other Celebrations have a lot of people with photographers etc, then yes, there is nothing wrong with booking a photographer again, except this time it is with the casket and grieving family and friends. This still would be memorable for families when they look back on the pictures years and years in the future and share with other family members. Remember, it is always weddings and funerals that bring families together and memoralizing a Celebration of Life will bring comfort in years to come.

Chapter 2:1

Celebration of Life During a Pandemic

Losing a family member is one thing, but this pandemic has made it even worse. Depending on where you live, the Covid Restrictions at the time of a death, and sadly, which funeral home is used, has made it very difficult for family members to decide whether they should go ahead with a service or wait until a later date. Unfortunately, there are some funeral homes that are not abiding by the Covid Restrictions, which is at times understandable when trying to work with a devastated family and having the restrictions change so quickly. Who would have thought the day would come that a guest list for a Celebration of Life would ever be a thing?

Since this pandemic started, here in Calgary, AB, Celebrations of Life restrictions have been as low as 15 people at any given time, then we had 25, then 50, then 100. Then, 50 people if there were no checks for vaccinations or having a negative Covid test, or up to a certain percentage of people based on building capacity, and, I am sure that the restrictions will continue to change at any given time.

Personally, I think the biggest problem here is that families do not know how devastating and difficult it is to make so many decisions while already in distress and now adding Covid Restrictions to the mix. Putting a plan in place today will make it much easier during that time. Because I have been part of various Celebration of Life gatherings for most of the changes with the Covid Restrictions here in Calgary, AB, I personally have a plan. I have suggested to my family that if any of us die during Covid with various restrictions in place, that we as immediate family with very close friends can attend the Celebration of Life and live stream the service online for all other family and friends so they can still be a part of the Celebration. This would be followed by another Celebration of Life once Covid settles down and there are no restrictions (if such a thing is possible again), proposing either the anniversary of one's passing or on one's birthday.

Now, if I die first, they could do whatever they like because, it will already be stress free for me to the maximum (lol). Doing a guest list for a wedding was difficult enough, yet alone for a funeral is a task that I personally will pass on in advance.

Having this discussion today and understanding that Celebration of Life gatherings are not the same as how it was back in early 2020 and prior, will hopefully help families to make the right decision with a peace of mind ensuring everyone is safe.

In summary, having a "Celebration of Life" gives your family the opportunity to share their tribute and get the time to celebrate and express who you are to them together with family and friends near and far.

As a family, we celebrate births, birthdays, graduation, weddings, anniversaries, new jobs, and much more, so why not celebrate your life?

Refer to Workbook Page(s):
Religious Leader/s
Pages: 212-213

Celebration of Life Instructions
Pages: 241-247

Chapter 3

Having the Conversation

"Ladies and gentlemen, the Captain has turned on the fasten seat belt sign. We are now crossing a zone of turbulence. Please return to your seats and keep your seat belts fastened. Thank you."

Does your family know what to do during a crisis?

Do they know where to find your important documents?

Have you had that important conversation with your loved ones?

Before a plane takes off, there are emergency procedures that are always explained to all passengers aboard the aircraft, either from the flight attendants or a short video.

These explain the Exit Plan if there is an emergency or what to do in the case of an emergency. This all includes but not limited to:

- Locating the nearest Exit closest to you before takeoff.

- Floor level lighting that will guide you to the Exit in the case of an emergency.

- How to use the oxygen mask if the air pressure is low and the mask is released.

- Where to locate the life jacket under the seat.

- What is the bracing position and how to go into it.

Let's be honest, having the death conversation is the most difficult conversation for anyone to have, especially with our loved ones. The thought of dying is not an easy one and for some of us, just speaking about it makes us feel like we are going to die. But that is far from the truth.

In fact, not having the conversation at all is likely to cause more chaos, confusion, and other problems than when the conversation is had. Discussing the topic and putting a plan in place not only brings you peace of mind now but will also bring peace of mind to your family during a crisis.

Can you imagine being on a plane and what the situation would be like in an emergency with all the chaos and confusion? Just as the airlines, who are complete strangers, are preparing us for an emergency, this is exactly what we can do to save our family from the chaos and confusion that arises. Having the discussion and having a plan in place is an act of love that would never be forgotten.

With many people getting infected with Covid-19 and dying from it, one wonders what prior discussions and pre-planning could have been in place beforehand to avoid the expression of anguish we hear from loved ones. I hear over and over again how families wished they had had some kind of a plan in place if anyone in their home caught Covid-19, and what to do afterwards. Sadly, we also hear of loved ones who got sick and how quickly things turned out for the worse and there being absolutely no discussion or plan in place to help the family in the midst of their grief and instead, having to switch into reactive mode to figure things out.

What if a loved one had notes on their phone or in a notebook on what to do if they caught Covid-19 and eventually died? Would that bring back a loved one? No! Would that stop others from catching Covid? No! But it would possibly make the situation easier for those who are involved and left behind. Putting a plan in place serves as a guide that shows step-by-step directions to help those who have no clue what to do or cannot think straight during a traumatic situation.

Interestingly, depending on where you live, Lawyers have commented how busy they are with clients coming in to get their Wills and other legal documents in place in case something happens. Insurance Agents are saying that old potential clients are contacting them to set up their policies just in case something happens. Hopefully, families would not have to need it, especially during the period of this pandemic, but if they do, the protections are set up.

This is why it is so important to have a conversation with our loved ones, as difficult as it sounds, to guide them on what to do during one of the most challenging times in their lives. Having the important discussion covers so many topics, including:

- Senior care options.

- Do Not Resuscitate Order (DNR) (may have a different name where you live).

- Whether you want your organs donated or not.

- Final disposition wishes.

- Where to find important documents.

- What to do with your stuff (Property and belongings).

Chapter 3:1

Do Not Resuscitate Order (DNR)

In chapters to come, there is additional information for each of the above except for the Do Not Resuscitate Order (DNR). This is one of the most difficult topics to discuss. A DNR order is pretty much a legally binding order signed by a physician at a patient's request letting medical professionals know one does not want to be resuscitated if one goes into cardiac arrest or stops breathing. For some, it is common sense that they would definitely want to be resuscitated. Now, this order is made when one patient is very clear about what they would or would not want in the event of a crisis in advance.

For example, if one goes into cardiac arrest or stops breathing, and it is clear that they are brain dead and will be in a vegetative state for extended periods or for the rest of their life, a decision needs to be made. Some people do not want to be a burden on their family or really do not want to live their last days in such a state, so if that is their option, they would rather end their life earlier. This is an exceedingly difficult situation when the family is left to make the decision to authorise the medical team to end one's life.

No words can explain the turmoil, the confusion, the guilt, the regret, the possible family breakdowns that a family is faced with when they have to make this decision but do not know what their loved one really wanted. Having this discussion on what your wishes are is crucial and needs to be had in all homes.

Think of the process in terms of being on a plane and knowing what to do during an emergency, as opposed to being on a plane and not knowing what to do during the emergency, except that this is a much worse situation.

When you think about this question for yourself when not in a crisis, what would you choose? Some decisions, at times, are made in a crisis and in most times, the decision would have been made differently, if it were discussed prior.

Whatever your decision is, ensure that it is known to your family or have the discussion with them but hope that such a crisis never happens. Speaking to medical professionals in your jurisdiction or your family physician will help you fully understand the Do Not Resuscitate (DNR) Order.

Chapter 3:2

Starting the Conversation

Depending on your loved ones, a few will have no problem talking about one's final wishes and what to do if one passes away. But in many cases, they will not want anything to do with such conversation. Or the flip side, you might want to know what your loved one's final wishes are. For example, your parents might not want to have the conversation. Or there are parents who want to have the discussion with their children but just do not know how to bring it up.

So, the big question is, how do we start this conversation?

Based on my experience, it is better to start a conversation with yourself.

For example, "I just want you to know that if I die or if I do not wake up tomorrow morning, I have taken care of everything in advance. Go underneath my bed and there you will find a suitcase with all my paperwork that you will need to help you through that difficult time. In the suitcase you will find information for the funeral home, cemetery contact details, my Will, insurance paperwork, and other pertinent documents.

There is a book called *"Final Departure"*; at the back of the book, I wrote down essential information that will help you at every stage, from the very beginning when I die, to what my final wishes are, to what I would like for my Celebration of Life and more."

From time to time, you can bring this up and once you can see that your family is comfortable with the topic, then you can start to go into details about your wishes. Let them know what your final wishes are: "I want to be buried/cremated. I want to donate my organs, I want you to have the painting in my room", and the list goes on.

It is important to find out what your loved ones' final wishes are and if they have a plan in place. Remember, whichever family member you do not know about, you will find out at the time of death. In some cases, it will be up to the family to figure it all out at that time. For example, if you or family members do not know whether a loved one wants to be buried or cremated, trying to figure it out during a crisis makes it more stressful during that difficult time.

It is like trying to get into the mind of a loved one who has passed away for information and it is completely impossible. This exacerbates the already difficult situation and opens possibilities for family disputes. Or, if you do not know if there is money or insurance in place to pay for the funeral home and/ or cemetery bill, it will be left to those who are left behind.

This is just the beginning of what happens when the conversation is not held beforehand.

Ideas on how to have the conversation are:

- Setting a time in your calendar and prioritizing to have the discussion (life happens, and it is so easy to not have the discussion).

- Attend a Celebration of Life Service with a loved one and start the conversation on what you liked about the service and what you would like for yours.

- Watch a movie (example: Departures, Get Low, Madea Family Funeral, Four Weddings and a Funeral and Death at a Funeral), some of these are really funny and is a great way to start the conversation.

- Attend, with a loved one, one of our Webinars/Seminars "Getting Your Affairs In Order," and, if you like, you can ask questions during the Q and A section so that they can hear the importance of having a plan in place before a crisis.

Having the conversation today will bring peace of mind to you and your loved ones in the long run. A plan will ensure less confusion and chaos at the time of a passing.

Chapter 4

Final Wishes for Disposition

What are your final wishes; to be buried or to be cremated?

Do you know the final disposition options available where you live?

Does your family know what your final wishes are between burial and cremation?

In retrospect, I think about when I worked with a unionized company, I would visit union members' homes to discuss their options for permanent benefits, including a funeral package. I could guarantee on a weekly basis that one of the husbands would tell me that his family could just put him in a box and bury him in the back. Of course, we would all laugh and even though it sounded very weird to me, I learned later on that legally, that is NOT an option in Canada. In fact, the options in Canada include burial in a cemetery or mausoleum or cremation. Yet, in other countries such as Africa or the Caribbean, being buried in the backyard or on family land is not a problem. It is only in later years that in certain places in Africa or the Caribbean that families are not burying loved ones on family land because the land is harder to sell; this is one of the main reasons.

Your final disposition wish is a statement or conversation of your dying wishes and instructions that your family will follow in the event of your death and what to do with your remains. In most countries, the options are cremation or burial. But, in the last few years, alkaline hydrolysis (bio-cremation) also known as aquamation, has become an option but is not offered in many places as of yet. Some of the places that are offering this option to families are St. Petersburg, Florida, United States; Ontario, Canada; and in South Africa.

Cremation

A process of reducing the body to bone fragments by applying intense heat for a period of two to three hours. The cremated remains are then removed from the cremation chamber and processed into finer fragments to be placed in a temporary container and then can be transferred to a more permanent container called an urn which holds the cremated remains.

Burial

The act or ceremony of putting human remains into a grave below ground in a cemetery or above ground in a mausoleum which is a large building that provides above ground options.

Alkaline hydrolysis, bio-cremation, or aquamation

Involves heating the body in heated water and potassium hydroxide, leaving only bones behind. The bones are then rinsed in the solution, dried, and reduced to small particles of ashes. This process is an alternative to cremation using water and chemicals instead of fire.

Working as a Licensed Pre-planning Specialist for many years has opened my eyes to people's varying preferences. The choices can be based on cultural and/or religious traditions, values, and sometimes based on pressure from other family members and friends.

But what is your final disposition wish?

I also think about when my cousin Nadine, a nurse based in Montreal, Quebec, had a patient who passed away in the hospital.

Traditionally, the Middle Eastern culture bury their loved one within three days from the time of death and the family was expecting their loved one's body to be released to them so they could go to the airport with the body. Unfortunately, this family was confident that it was not a problem for them to get the body, but to their shock they learned that by law they had to work with a funeral home first to be able to repatriate their loved one back home. I remember how upset my cousin was explaining the situation to me and how horrible it felt trying to explain it to the family and how they really struggled at first to understand how things work in Canada.

This is a perfect example of being in a crisis and not being able to think rationally. What was more puzzling to me was how they were going to get their loved one in the car or even worse, on the plane.

It is important to know the various ways our final disposition can affect those left behind. While some members of the family would prefer to not look in the casket, others may need to see their loved one in order to say their final goodbye. Therefore, it is important to have a conversation with our loved ones to see what they might need for their peace of mind before a death.

Chapter 4:1

Cremation

Oftentimes, Funeral Directors tell me how families contact the funeral home wanting to see their loved one and they have to break the news that their loved one has already been cremated. Please keep in mind that depending on the funeral parlor, cremation can be done after loved ones get their final chance to pay their final respects.

Note that if you tell your loved ones that you want to be cremated, that could mean three different options and sometimes causes a lot of confusion once families go to the funeral parlor. The cremation options are: a direct cremation, a memorial, or a traditional funeral followed by a cremation.

Direct cremation is when one passes away and comes into the care of the funeral parlor to be directly cremated with no service. Yes, there might be a viewing for identification but that is it. Soon after, the family returns and picks up the cremated remains.

Memorial is when one passes away and comes into the care of the funeral parlor to be directly cremated followed by a Celebration of Life Service at the funeral parlor or anywhere else of choice.

Traditional funeral followed by a cremation is a service with the body present in a rented casket at the funeral parlor/church or elsewhere followed by a cremation after the Celebration of Life Service. In this case, instead of the coach/hearse going to the cemetery following the service, the loved one is brought back to the funeral parlor for cremation.

Overall, don't forget to mention to your loved ones what to do with your cremated remains. In some cases, after the body has been cremated, there is great confusion on what to do next.

There are several options regarding use of cremated remains:

- Put in an urn (wood, marble, metal, ceramic).

- Burial at a cemetery below ground or above ground in niche or in an indoor mausoleum.

- Used in jewellery (ring or necklace).

- Handcrafted into a beautiful keepsake of your choice in your favorite color scheme through glass blowing. (e.g., Christmas tree ornament, paperweight, various shapes).

- Scattering (cemeteries, ocean).

Depending on where you live, there are things that can and cannot be done with cremated remains so don't forget to ask your funeral director in your jurisdiction.

Many of us have heard about loved ones wanting to be scattered in different countries or scattered in different places.

I just want to shed light on this based on a story that I heard not too long ago. Keep in mind that as lovely as having to scatter cremated remains in different places by your loved ones sounds like an amazing idea, it is sometimes more difficult for a family member to actually grant such a wish. In each instance, loved ones saddled with such responsibility would have to build up the courage to go to a different place to scatter the ashes.

This is not an easy task, emotionally, psychologically, physically, or otherwise. This too is something to talk about in advance and to possibly let your loved ones know that even though it is your final wish, if it does not get done, it is okay. Some of the final wishes that are left for loved ones to carry can affect them in the long run more than one can ever imagine.

Chapter 4:2

Burial

Burial options would be with a casket present at the "Celebration of Life" followed by a burial at a cemetery or mausoleum or even a graveside service followed by a burial. In recent years, another option of burial is a green burial or natural burial in which the interment of the human remains are put in the soil in a manner that does not cause problems for decomposition but instead allows the human remains to be naturally recycled. In this case, there is no metal, plastic or embalming of the human remains buried in the ground.

Caskets

With burial as an option for final disposition, there are a few additional product selections that need to be decided on. The primary one is choosing a casket. Choosing a casket can be quite the task but starting with whether the preference is wood or metal will start to narrow down the options.

Wood caskets can come in walnut, pine, oak, maple, elm, pecan, mahogany, etc., while metal caskets can come in copper, bronze, carbon steel, stainless steel, etc. Although the interior parts of the caskets can have various light colors, caskets can also be customized using additional decorations such as the corners of the casket or personalized panel which is inside the top of the casket. In fact, one of the funeral homes I work with, customized a casket for a mother, whose son's favorite football team was the Kansas City Chiefs. The casket looked amazing with the red and gold colors and meant the world to this mother. Overall, having an idea in advance of what your choices and budget are, will assist with making a good decision.

Interestingly enough, some countries in Africa have caskets of all shapes and sizes. I have seen cars, airplanes, Coca-Cola bottles, animals, shoes, and the list goes on, which personalizes the casket to the one who passes away.

Chapter 4:3

Memorialization

One of the most important parts of losing a loved one is being able to memorialize them.

Memorialization is the comforting place where family and friends can go to remember, pay tribute, and honor their loved one. Depending on where you live, there are many options such as:

- Burial in a cemetery or mausoleum.

- Name being engraved on a memorial park bench.

- Plant a tree with a plaque in front.

- Name engraved on some type of a monument at the cemetery where your loved one was buried.

Other options to memorialize a family member besides going to a comforting place are:

- Setting up an honorary scholarship.

- Contribute to a local charity or a church.

- Have a special day every year to do something that your loved one enjoyed doing.

Memorializing a loved one can be made beautiful and will be comforting for years to come.

**Refer to Workbook Page(s):
Funeral Home and Cemetery Contact Details
Pages: 201-202**

Chapter 5

Wills and Living Wills

Do you have a Will?

Do you know why a Will is so important?

Do you have other legal documents in place (Living Wills), in the event of losing mental capacity, due to an accident or illnesses such as Dementia or Alzheimer's Disease?

Having a Will and Living Wills (in the event you lose mental capacity) in place are very crucial. However, many people do not fully understand the importance of these documents.
Statistically, about 60% of Canadians and Americans do not have a Will, this varies from city, province/state, and country but is definitely worth researching. That does not include those who have not updated their Wills to reflect current life changes.

Have you ever contacted your telephone company and they were not able to verify your identity?

How horrible did that feel?

When someone passes away and a family member or someone tries to call the telephone company to close the account over the phone, the representative would keep insisting that they need to talk to the account holder. This is a nightmare that people must endure that is exacerbated by not having a Will that gives the Executor the authority to deal with the deceased's bills and accounts. Not to mention in some cases, the horrible experience of going in person to stand in line with the death certificate. Again, in many cases, nothing can be done until someone is appointed to deal with the deceased's estate. If there was a Will, the deceased would have appointed someone they trust to be the Executor in charge of their estate and there would be fewer to no problems.

Could you imagine what would happen to your family's bills if no one had authority while they wait for the court to move through their processes? What would happen if there were no joint bank accounts allowing your surviving partner or spouse access to pay these bills? This could mean placing everything on hold until someone is appointed by the courts.

Chapter 5:1

What is a Will

A Will is a legal document that states our final wishes. It allows us to divide up our property and many of the things we own. It also allows us to indicate what to do with our minor children, if we have any, when we pass away. Having a Will is our voice when we are no longer around. I mention minor children for a reason. Prior to being a Licensed Pre-Planning Specialist, I worked with a unionized company where I would visit union members' homes to explain to them their options for permanent benefits. I often asked the union members if they had a Will created and the common response was a resounding No.

On reflection, I too must admit that I did not have a Will, therefore the responses were not surprising. Until I had an encounter with a young couple that changed everything!

One day I visited a young couple's home and when I asked if they had a Will, I was shocked when they told me yes. When asked why they had a Will, they told me it was because of an experience at the funeral of a close family friend who died from domestic violence.

To their surprise, the children attended the funeral in the company of Alberta Children's Services (social services) – the mother had no Will in place at the time of death, so the government department stepped in and took custody of the children.

This is one of my main reasons why having a Will should be considered a matter of necessity - a Will is pretty much our mouthpiece when we are no longer around to state our intentions regarding our children or our financial affairs.

Having a Will allows you to appoint someone to carry out your wishes and intentions when you die. When you die without a Will, it means that you have died intestate. Yes, that means that before anyone can step in and make decisions on your behalf, the appointment of the person must be approved by the courts. This is where provincial legislation dictates who has priority to apply to be that individual who deals with your estate and wraps up your financial affairs on your behalf. The court process can often take several months or years, and it depends on the law in your city, province/state, and country.

Chapter 5:2

Who is an Executor (Personal Representative)?

An Executor (Personal Representative) depending on who it is called in your jurisdiction, is the person named in the Will who is legally responsible to carry out the directions contained in the Will.

When we have a Will and have appointed an Executor, the Will gives the Executor the legal authority to deal with our estate. On occasion, this allows the Executor to deal with matters right away, after a loved one has passed away.

In other instances, the Executor may have to probate the Will, which is a court process that verifies the Will. In either case, it is only the Executor that can contact our financial institution(s), telephone and/or utility companies etc. if it is not a joint account. Without a Will, no one has immediate authority and access to our accounts or affairs and are firmly denied.

Often dealing with a loved one's estate, or settling an estate, can take upwards of a year or more. It can even be longer, depending on the laws and processes in our jurisdiction, when there is no Will in place. One of the hardest things to accept about death is the finality of it and not having access to information anymore through a simple conversation dialogue.

Having a Will brings comfort to your family and loved ones because even though you are gone, you have left them with the peace of mind knowing that there are written instructions on how to proceed and what to do, especially when they have no clue what to do.

Chapter 5:3

Executor (Personal Representative) Ideal Characteristics

As mentioned above, part of preparing a Will is choosing the right Executor. At times, this can be difficult, so here are a few pointers for choosing an Executor.

Not only should we choose an Executor, but we should also select an alternative in case our first choice cannot function as our Executor. In fact, some lawyers also advise having an odd number of Executors to make the decision-breaker easier when it comes to making decisions. Or, if there are more than two children, always choose more than two to be the Executor.

Ideal Characteristics are:

- Trustworthy and honest.

- Living in close geographical proximity to us (lives in same city or province/state).

- Younger than us or someone that is mature with an awareness of the responsibility of being an Executor.

- Impartial in their treatment and views of others: fair and equitable.

- Financially savvy.

- Available and have the time to undergo the estate process.

- Able to make decisions based on similar morals and values as us.

Chapter 5:4

Executor (Personal Representative) Responsibilities

I remember the days when I thought being an Executor, also referred to as a Personal Representative, here in Alberta, Canada was considered an honor, until I changed careers.

Now, the number one question I often hear is whether being an Executor/Personal Representative is a blessing or a curse? And, of course this is not a one-answer response as other factors must be considered. Whenever I am asked to be an Executor, I pose questions like:

Do you have life insurance in place to take care of your young child/ren in case you die prematurely? I have had to ask or suggest:

- It is not a good idea to appoint a minor child (a child who is under the age of 18) as a beneficiary on a life insurance policy, as those funds are held in trust until a specified age.

- Do you want to be cremated or buried?

A few of the core responsibilities of an Executor include but not limited to:

- Funeral arrangements.
- Safeguarding and protection of assets.
- Probating the Will and filing any necessary legal documents.
- Debt repayment.
- Filing taxes and getting clearance from taxing authorities.
- Informing and showing the accounting to all the beneficiaries.
- Getting releases signed by beneficiaries.
- Distributing the assets or setting up trusts.

Yes, funeral arrangements! The first thing that will be asked when a family goes to the funeral parlor after a death is whether there is a Will? This is important information for the funeral parlor because they want to know who the Executor is. The Executor has the last word and, in most cases, will be looked upon to pay the bill.

Protecting assets of the deceased is a huge responsibility. Therefore, valuable assets such as houses and cars, the immediate changing of locks, securing keys for vehicles, and confirming whether there are property and vehicle insurance in place are of utmost importance.

If there are others living in the home of the deceased, you may have to put locks in place or move items to a secured area.

Every situation will be different but securing items will make the process easier for the Executor and ensure that property does not get damaged or go missing. If you live alone, ensure you give a set of spare keys to your Executor, close friend, or family member, for your place of residence and for your vehicle(s).

Funeral bills will be a debt that has to be handled right away. All other debts of the deceased and tax payments will also need to be dealt with. Just remember that all debts of the deceased must be satisfied before there can be any distribution of the deceased's assets to the beneficiaries. So, the more debts there are, the less money will be left to the beneficiaries. This is another reason why life insurance is so important, which will be discussed in another chapter.

Did you know that the Executor, at times, can be responsible for maintaining and paying bills out of their pocket?

If the Executor has access to the deceased's funds, then the deceased's funds are used to maintain the bills. But mostly, the Executor will not have access to the deceased's funds until after Grant of Probate is received. So, if the Executor cannot access the deceased's funds, then the Executor uses their own money, and then will eventually reimburse themselves from the deceased's funds when there is access.

If the Executor doesn't have the funds themselves, then those bills go unpaid.

Even though there could be many calls from creditors, if there is not enough money in the estate to manage those debts, the Executor will not be responsible to pay off those debts with their own money. Those debts will be paid from the estate.

Overall, this is where the Executor can decide which bills are important to maintain in the long run. Foreclosure can be the result if mortgage payments go unpaid.

Please note, this is different if there is another person who is joint on that debt or bill. For example, if a couple has a joint credit card in both of their names, the surviving spouse would be responsible for payment of the remaining balance. This is where it may be worth considering having separate credit cards or lines of credit in individual names, rather than jointly, whenever possible.

It is also the Executor or the Personal Representative's responsibility who is appointed where there is a Will, to commence any court proceedings. Filing legal documents can be stressful especially when it is unfamiliar territory and errors are made resulting in the courts rejecting the application. To give you an example, in Alberta, there can be as many as 19 documents, sometimes more or less, depending on the circumstances of each estate to be completed and filed. If there are any errors, the court may reject the application and return them for corrections.

It would be best to have a conversation with a Wills and Estate Lawyer in your jurisdiction and they would provide the most suitable advice on the legal requirements of each estate. Your Executor may determine the sections that they can complete and areas where a legal expert is required. Of course, having a Lawyer complete the administration or settlement of the estate, from the beginning, may eradicate or eliminate unnecessary delays.

Another responsibility of the Executor is keeping all beneficiaries informed about proceedings and providing financial reporting. An accounting shows the beneficiaries the value of the estate, what amounts were paid out for bills and expenses for settling the estate, and what amounts were collected, to arrive at a final balance of what is left in the estate for distribution. As you can imagine, there are times where beneficiaries may expect an inheritance, but because of the debts, they may receive little or nothing from the estate. Keep in mind that giving beneficiaries an estimate on how long the process can take, and what steps are being taken, may alleviate some of the beneficiaries' stress which could lessen your stress as well.

Once debts are paid, including tax authorities, and a clearance is given, Executors often provide the accounting to the beneficiaries to get their approval. Releases are signed by the beneficiaries, and then distribution of assets can finally happen.
The distribution must be in accordance with intestate legislation if there is no Will. If there is a Will, the distribution must be in

accordance with the Will. If the Will requires the setup of any trusts, then trusts can now be created for the beneficiaries.

It is in your best interest to find a good Lawyer who specializes in Wills and Estates to get proper advice. While there are options to get a Will Kit, or complete a do-it-yourself Will online, using such services may not provide the right protection to loved ones in the long run. Again, it is best to consult with an experienced Wills and Estates Lawyer since laws are different depending on your jurisdiction, and all family dynamics are different.

I always say, we get what we pay for – collaborating with a Lawyer who specializes in Wills and Estates is worth every penny. Just remember that it is hard to get a deceased person to cooperate, as they are no longer around to verify or clarify information or receive guidance on any proceedings. Hiring an experienced Lawyer from the beginning will reduce the chance of a Will being contested or having difficulties with the court process.

The aim is to avoid chaos amongst your family and loved ones and not having to deal with problems that could have been identified before the passing of a beloved family member. Some estates are basic while others can be much more complicated. A perfect example of a complicated situation in estates is where there is a blended family. A blended family is a family where the spouses or partners have children from previous relationships and now they have combined to form a new family. Any person in a related situation should consult with an experienced Wills and Estates Lawyer who specializes in estates where there are blended families to get their Will completed properly so the division of assets will be distributed fairly amongst all children after the last partner or spouse passes away.

Chapter 5:5

Bank Account

It may appear that having a joint bank account with a child, or a spouse is a good option. But be careful, because these accounts bring their own problems, and one size may not fit all. There are pros and cons to joint bank accounts, and we should get legal advice from an trusted Wills and Estates Lawyer before making any of our accounts joint with another person. Sometimes we can end up fixing one mistake, but it introduces a whole new set of problems.

An option to consider when adding a child or spouse to the account is to add them as a beneficiary instead of being added to our account jointly. Some parents think to add their children to their account so if they pass away, money is available to manage final arrangements. Adding a loved one to our account jointly gives them full access to our funds, as well as creditors, to go into the account if they owe money, especially if our loved one is banking personally at the same bank. Adding a loved one as a beneficiary gives them access to our account when we die.

Chapter 5:6

Common-Law Spouse

What is a common-law spouse?

A common-law spouse (also called common-law partner or common-law marriage, common-law couple or adult interdependent partners) generally means a couple who live together in a marriage-like relationship but are not legally married. Depending on the province/state and country, an unmarried couple is considered common-law if they have cohabited - lived together in a conjugal relationship - continuously for a given period of time. For example, in British Columbia, Canada, a couple needs to have been in a conjugal relationship for at least two years. However, there are many exceptions.

Why is this so important?

This is important for a number of reasons. If a common-law partner passes away, it means that the surviving common-law partner could possibly be the beneficiary of the deceased's estate if there is no Will in place. What happens if the deceased has no children but has parents, siblings, nieces, and nephews? What happens to their estate? This largely depends on where one lives and subsisting laws. Without a Will in place, things can easily spin out of control and cause a lot of confusion with potentially serious consequences.

If you are in a common-law relationship or know someone who is, it is advised to do some research and ask a Wills and Estate Lawyer in your area specific questions like:

- When is a couple considered to be in a common-law relationship?

- What are your rights when a partner moves into one's property? What does one stand to lose if a partner moves in?

- If one falls sick and there is no living will (if one loses mental capacity), who is responsible for making decisions on their behalf?

- If one passes away, what happens to their estate/personal belongings when there is no Will in place?

- What happens when there is a Will in place?

- What can I do to protect my estate and ensure that family or those whom I want to be beneficiaries are properly set up?

Having a properly documented Will done by an experienced Wills and Estates Lawyer will help ensure that one's situation will be properly assessed before drawing up a Will that will help ensure that their wishes will be carried through at the time of death. Keeping in mind that there are situations where the Will can be overruled, in cases like joint tenancy on a property or already delegated beneficiaries who were not updated.

This is the kind of situation that Wills and Estates Lawyers see on a regular basis, especially when it comes to separated or divorced spouses who do not update their documents. Situations like this leaves adult child/ren trying to maintain the bills etc., while this gets fixed and could take months or years to rectify. Speaking with an experienced Will and Estates Lawyer will help to pick up on these missed updates that one might have innocently missed.

Chapter 5:7

Holograph Wills

For some, a Holograph Will is a temporary option until a properly drafted Will is completed by your Lawyer. A Holograph Will is a Will that's done entirely in your own handwriting, and it documents your final wishes and distribution of your assets. Even though this can be the most cost-effective option out there, bear in mind that you get what you pay for. Depending on the situation, the Will may or may not be valid. We see this in cases where a child cannot prove that the document was done in their parent's own handwriting.

There may be certain provinces/states or countries that do not accept a Holograph Will. It's best to consult with a Lawyer in your area to see if a Holographic Will would be recognized as a valid Will in your jurisdiction. In situations like this, it is advisable to consult with two to three Lawyers to ensure you are getting accurate information. Remember, there is no possibility to fix or amend a Will if death occurs, so at times, it is better to be safe than sorry.

A situation I was recently notified of is a perfect example of why it is better to be safe than sorry when it comes to Holograph Wills. Having a properly drafted Will prepared by an qualified Wills and Estate Lawyer would have been the first step in avoiding this common error which led to devastating consequences. These are common stories that Wills and Estate Lawyers see on a regular basis.

Unfortunately, a mother was dying of cancer and one of her adult sons quit his job and moved in to help and take care of her. At some point, she decided to do up a Holograph Will, stating her intentions for her house and accounts to go to her two adult sons. Mom passes away and the sons go to the Lawyer's office to start working on her estate. What they found out was the house was still in joint names (as joint tenants) between mom and her estranged husband. This meant that the house was not part of mom's estate. The house would automatically pass outside of mom's estate directly to the surviving joint owner, which means the estranged husband now is the sole owner of the house. The mom's registered retirement saving plan (RRSP) had also named the estranged husband as the beneficiary. When there is a named beneficiary on a RRSP, the RRSP gets paid to the named beneficiary and is NOT part of the mom's estate. What people don't realize is that your Will only distributes assets that are INSIDE an estate, and a house with a surviving joint owner (in a joint tenancy) passes OUTSIDE the estate.

A RRSP with a surviving named beneficiary on the account passes OUTSIDE the estate. In other words, the Will had no ability to deal with the house or the RRSP. They were both outside of the control of the Will.

To make matters even worse, the estranged husband who got the house and the RRSP proceeds was living in a care facility suffering from dementia.

How was the son, who was without a job and who just lost his mom, to maintain the house? There was no money INSIDE the estate for him to use. All the assets were OUTSIDE the estate in the hands of an estranged husband who had no mental capacity. Are we seeing what a mess this is? This devastated son, who has dropped everything to help his mother, is now in a horrible position that could have been avoided if the mom had received proper advice and not taken the easiest or cheapest route. Unfortunately for these sons, the only way they will receive anything from the house is if mom's estranged husband (who also happened to be the sons' father) dies. This also depends on whether the estranged husband has a Will himself leaving these assets to the sons (or if the estranged husband died intestate and the province's laws deem the sons to be the beneficiaries of his estate).

Remember, speaking with a Wills and Estates Lawyer where you live will be the best place to understand the laws and regulations in your jurisdiction. In some cases, every province/state and country have different rules and is not a one shoe-fits-all.

Lastly, if you plan to put your Will in a safety deposit box at your bank, ensure your Executor knows where to find the key for the box in order to retrieve your Will.

As my friend and Estate Lawyer, Angela Yee-Hamshaw, would say *"Where there's a Will, a properly drafted Will, there's a way!"*

Chapter 5:8

Living Wills

There are two other legal documents that all adults should have. These documents come into effect if one loses mental capacity, due to an accident or illness like Dementia or Alzheimer's Disease.

Living Will 1 - Allows one to appoint someone they trust to oversee their financial affairs.

Living Will 2 - Allows one to appoint someone they trust to oversee their medical and personal affairs.

These legal documents appoint someone in advance to take care of you or your affairs if you lose mental capacity. These documents should not be confused with a Will. A Will only takes effect at the time of death. The other two legal documents are used whilst alive. However, if you have lost mental capacity these remain in effect until you are competent to commence making your own decisions, or until one passes away, at which point the Will goes into effect.

In Alberta, the Enduring Power of Attorney is used to oversee financial affairs and the Personal Directive, is for personal and medical decisions. Each province in Canada or state in the

United States has similar documents however, they may have different names. Another point to note is that the individuals appointed may be revoked at any time, hence the recommendation is to review these documents periodically throughout your life stage.

Pre-planning who you want to make decisions on your behalf if you lose mental capacity allows you to make important decisions on a normal day when you are not faced with a crisis.

Pre-planning gives you the opportunity to make that decision on your own. If these documents are not prepared in advance of losing mental capacity, then the court becomes involved. A family member would need to apply to the court to be appointed to receive authority to make decisions on your behalf. The danger is that it could be a family member you would never entrust to make those financial or medical decisions on your behalf. For example, if you have a son or daughter who does not manage finances well, it could be that very child applying to have decision-making power over your finances. Just imagine, knowing you have a specific child you would not want to touch your finances with a ten-foot pole, and now because you failed to plan ahead, they are the individuals appointed by the courts. If this is not settling, putting a plan in place today will avoid a situation like this.

Planning in advance not only allows you to appoint someone you trust and know they have your best interest at heart, but it will also save your family money in the long run. Not appointing someone in advance will add emotional and mental stress to an already devastated family. This can be a very tedious process to deal with through the courts, depending on where you live. We hear of many cases of loved ones passing away while waiting for the court order to be in place.

Many Lawyers will offer these three documents as a package, the Will and two Living Wills. In the long run, having these documents in place can save you and your loved one's thousands of dollars and will give everyone peace of mind during a crisis.

**Refer to Workbook Page(s):
Important Documents Log
Pages: 214-224**

Chapter 6

Insurance

Do you have dependents who rely on you financially?

Do you have Insurance to cover your paycheck if you die prematurely?

Does your personal insurance cover your final/funeral expenses even after retirement?

This topic alone has caused a lot of confusion at the time of one's passing and will continue to cause confusion if we do not understand the various insurance products available.

After speaking with various funeral directors in Canada and the U.S, the main problem they consistently see when family members come to prepare final arrangements was no surprise to me.

I am sure you guessed it right. Besides not having the conversation and knowing what their loved one wanted, the next big issue is the funds needed to pay the funeral home.

When it comes to insurance policies, loved ones at the time of need, are sometimes faced with one of the following:

- Policy lapsed or cancelled.

- Unable to find the paperwork.

- Term insurance product has ended.

- Accidental Death policy not being paid out when death is deemed as a natural cause.

- No insurance.

As uncomfortable as this is, especially when it comes to our parents, asking all loved ones and getting an idea who has coverage amongst each family member will save a lot of surprises when arriving at the funeral parlor. Realizing that someone must pay for this immediate expense is a surprise to many. At this point, it is no longer the problem of the deceased but those who are left behind.

There are cases where family members have taken on the payment or owning the policy of a loved one. Understanding that if something happens to the insured, the responsibility falls on them. This is especially true when children or spouses are involved, and one knows the potential of nothing being in place if something happens.

Remember, having an insurance policy and naming a beneficiary on the policy protects your family from any debts you have. Debts you have must be repaid from your estate before any money goes to your family. If you die and have nothing in your estate, then your debts die with you as they cannot be repaid.

Your estate is all the property, goods, and money that you own. Thankfully, in most cases, depending on where you live, your relatives do not have to pay off your debts unless they have provided personal guarantees for those debts or if the debt is joint with someone else.

Insurance policies pay your beneficiaries a direct tax-free cash payout that they can use for whatever they need. This money can help cover daily expenses, ease financial burdens, and pay for those goals you've worked so hard together as a family to achieve.

Overall, having an insurance policy can protect your family from financial hardship when you are no longer around.

Let's briefly go through the various products out there so that we can compare our own personal products and ask the right questions in advance before it is too late.

Chapter 6:1

Term Insurance Policy

This product is like paycheck protection and it's ideal if someone dies before retirement. Term insurance policies are typically for 10, 20 or 30 years. When the term is over, it can either be non-renewable or renewed up to a certain age for example 65 or 75 years before it usually expires at the age of 85 years. This product is highly recommended for any adult and will be there to take care of our family if we die and our paycheck is no longer coming in to support the family. The reason why this insurance is reasonably priced is because only 2-4% of this product pays out because most of us outlive our term insurance policy.

Surviving our insurance is ideal because our family would prefer for us to be around but just in case that does not happen, our family will be taken care of. Yes, having this product is important.

When I first started learning about various insurance products, I remembered hearing people say, 'I am worth more dead than alive,' due to owning some insurance product(s). But now that I fully understand how these products work, I find such comments not accurate, because our family would rather have us around any day than the money.

In most cases, depending on the policy, this insurance is non-existent if we pass away in our later years because we outlive the insurance policy.

Another term insurance policy is our work insurance products. If we get laid off, quit, or retire, we no longer have insurance coverage. Having our own term life policy along with our work insurance products are ideal up until we retire. Planning in advance for other investments, savings, or insurance products to cover our final expenses such as funeral parlor, cemetery bills and taxes after our term products have ended will relieve those financial burdens from our family.

Term insurance is known as renting the policy and the option to convert to a permanent product up to a certain age. If you have any questions on this product, please contact an insurance agent in your area and speak with two to three agents in your area to get clarity and a better understanding before cancelling or renewing your products.

Chapter 6:2

Whole Life Policy

This product is ideal for our legacy and final expenses because it will be there when one passes away. Unlike term insurance, we own this product, and it should be there for life. Please note that one of the reasons why this would not pay or only a portion of it would pay out at the time of death is because the option to borrow from this policy is available.

There are various options for this type of product which include;

- Paying for it until you die or to the age 100.
- Paying for it until a set time like 10 or 20 years.
- Having dividends on it to bring up the value of the policy.
- Having the opportunity to offset premiums with dividends.

If you have any questions on this product, please contact an insurance agent in your area and speak with two to three agents in your area to get clarity and a better understanding before canceling or renewing your products.

Chapter 6:3

Universal Life Policy

There are two payment options for a Universal Life Policy

1. Level Cost

2. Increasing Cost

Most of the Universal Life Policies that are sold fall under the increasing cost category hence the reason why I personally steer far away from this product.

I dare not talk too much about this product for numerous reasons. If this product is not set up properly by an experienced agent, the possibility of this product being manageable during our senior years are minimal to non-existent. Please ask questions and try to fully understand this product before deciding to add it to your portfolio. If you are not confident with this product and do not fully understand it, please do whatever it takes to understand it including looking at the information at the back of the policy.

My personal advice on this product is that if you own this product, you should be monitoring it as much as your agent and understand how this product works, especially long term. I have seen in numerous cases where seniors have been paying into this product and had to cancel it or had it lapse because they no longer have the funds to maintain it. This essentially means that they placed "all their eggs in one basket," and they are not able to retrieve all those funds which could have been invested into another product or perhaps their retirement savings. Choose carefully when it comes to this product and even ask your insurance agent how long they have been selling this product.

If you have any questions on this product, please contact an insurance agent in your area and speak with two to three agents in your area to get clarity and a better understanding before cancelling or renewing your products.

Chapter 6:4

Pre-Need Insurance Policy (Funeral Home Prepaid Policy)

This product is specifically for funeral homes that combines the funding and final wishes with a specific funeral home. As with everything else, the cost of funeral home prices increases every year and having this product in advance guarantees the cost at the funeral home of your choice. The additional advantage of this insurance product is that it's locked in and guarantees today's dollars, therefore offering peace of mind. This secures family members not having to pay the funeral home bill out of pocket. The funeral home is the beneficiary for this policy; therefore, it allows them to be paid within 1-2 business days.

With this type of insurance, you can do as little as you like or as much as you like, such as:

- Choosing your preferred funeral home.

- Open a file for yourself and/or another family member.

- Complete your vital statistics (information the government requires before a death certificate is issued at the time of death).

- Your choice of disposition is selected (cremation or burial).

- Payment for the funeral home bill can be paid monthly, lump-sum payments, or in full, years and years before needed.

Overall, setting up the Pre-Need Insurance Policy in advance will be a tremendous help and relief to your family as it removes the difficult task of them trying to decide on which funeral home to contact whilst trying to come to terms with your passing.

If you have any questions on this product, visit a funeral home near you or speak to a Pre-planning Specialist like myself who has working relationships with a funeral home.

Chapter 6:5

Worldwide Travel Protection Policy

This product is a repatriation coverage for those who pass away whilst travelling. This item is a peace of mind product because if a death happens 100km outside of our primary residence, this product will bring our remains home to our loved ones at no extra cost. Losing a loved one at home is difficult enough, however, to lose a loved one whilst in another country magnifies the grieving process not to mention navigating varying country laws and regulations. Having this coverage will make a world of a difference during a devastating event.

With this coverage, our family contacts the number on the card and they take care of the rest of the process. Hopefully, our family will never need to use this product, however, it is available if they need it.

Having a Worldwide Travel Protection Insurance Coverage:

- Ensures that the closest funeral home at the time of death is contacted.

- Covers the funeral home cost (preparation of the body, embalming, appropriate minimal container for transportation and shipping costs).

- Covers consulate fees and government regulation fees if applicable.

- Covers the airline cost.

The exorbitant cost and struggle to return a loved one from another Country can be a nightmare that it's negative effects can last a lifetime. Repatriation fees can be high; therefore, many families resort to cremating their loved ones abroad before bringing their remains home. In most cases, a lot of people have travel insurance but would have to pay all the cost upfront for repatriation before submitting receipts and receiving the money back.

Our advice is to contact your insurance company and ask them specific questions, for e.g., if a loved one passes away while on vacation, would they pay the funeral home and airline fees directly? Repatriation fees and the stress that comes with it during a devastating time is nothing to take lightly. This can be a very unpleasant task for families.

For more information, visit a funeral home near you or speak to a Pre-planning Specialist like myself who has working relationships with a funeral home.

Chapter 6:6

Accidental Death and Dismemberment Policy

This type of policy is typically sold separately at a bank or insurance company and advisable to be considered as an add-on to another policy for e.g., a term or whole life policy. The unfortunate part of this insurance policy is that if one dies from natural causes like a stroke, heart attack, cancer etc., this policy would not pay out to beneficiaries. This type of insurance only pays out if a death occurs from an accident or provides protection in the event of a loss of limb, sight, hearing, and/or speech due to an accidental injury.

Having this policy is a great add-on if you pass away from an accident, there will be additional funds for your loved ones. The biggest problem with having this product and nothing else is that if you die from natural causes, it will not pay out and will come as a surprise when families visit the funeral home with this certificate. Again, ask questions and learn about these products to ensure you have the right coverage.

Please ensure that you speak with an Insurance Agent to better understand this product that you have or plan on purchasing in the future.

If you have any questions on this product, please contact an insurance agent in your area and/or speak with two or three agents in your area to get clarity and a better understanding before cancelling or renewing your products.

Overall, your own personal insurance products should be as important, and in most cases, more important than your car, home, property insurance because it protects you personally.

Setting up your children as a rider on your own policy or with their own policy from a young age will save money, and possibly a deniable opportunity for insurance products later in life due to health or lifestyle choices. Insurance products premiums are based on age, sex, health, and smoking status. Locking in lower premium rates for individual policies primarily based on age will save thousands of dollars in the future.

As one of my business partners Glen Griffiths would say, "It is better to have insurance one day too early than one minute too late."

In summary, remember to:

1. Have a policy or money delegated to pay the funeral home and/or cemetery bill now and after retirement.

2. Review your policies and beneficiaries on a regular basis

including your personal and work insurance policies.

3. Add your child/ren as a rider on your policy at birth and set them up with their own policy at a young age.

4. Understanding what coverage is set up, so if something happens, there will be no surprises for your family during that difficult time.

Happy personal insurance product research!!!

Refer to Workbook Page(s):
Important Documents Log
Pages: 214-224

Chapter 7

Organ and Tissue Donation vs Body Donation

Do you want to donate your organs when you pass away?

Do you want to donate your body to a medical school?

Do you fully understand the difference between the two?

While organ and tissue donation and body donation to a medical school are considered life-giving and life-enhancing opportunities, they can come with a lot of confusion at the time of death when your wishes have not been clearly communicated with family in advance. Whatever is not discussed and registered is another surprise to family members, which undoubtedly adds to the devastation and may open up family conflict, along with your final wishes not being granted.

Clearly communicating your desire for organs and tissues to be donated and registering this with the city, province/state, or country will make a difference. Your local registry can help you with this or you can do this online, ensuring this information is shared with those who would need to know your intentions. It's important to remember that it depends on where you are as the process may be a little different in each city, province/state, or country.

The process of a body being donated to a medical school is quite different from organ and tissue donation.

Chapter 7:1

Organ and Tissue Donation

Organ and tissue donation often happens when a sudden death occurs as a result of trauma. One common example is when a trauma victim who is otherwise healthy passes away because of a motor vehicle collision.

When it is clear that the donor is going to die, the individual may be kept on life support until physicians can harvest the organs or tissue and be transferred to the qualified recipients.

The donation of organs is not always guaranteed. Many factors may surface to disqualify the candidate. The reasons for disqualification may vary. Our health care professionals understand the "value of the gift" of donation and do all in their power to harvest organs and tissue from qualified donors. Understanding this will help your family not to feel guilty in any way at the time of death.

In cases when the donor is healthy, there are certain medical exclusion criteria and non-medical exclusions that prevent organ donation. Researching this in advance and understanding what the medical exclusion criteria are and the non-medical exclusion criteria are in your jurisdiction will give you a good idea whether or not you are able to be a donor based on your situation now.

If you can be an organ donor based on your current health, you are halfway there.

At the time of a possible donation, while in the hospital, the family will be asked if their wishes are for the loved one to be a donor. At times the system is checked in advance to see if that person's request is on file. Upon completion of the harvesting, the funeral home is contacted to care for the loved one and the family can continue with final funeral arrangements.

Please note that organ donation is only possible when the donor has died in the hospital. Organs need a supply of oxygen-rich blood to remain suitable for transplantation. On the flip side, tissue donation is usually possible if the donor dies in a non-hospital setting.

Chapter 7:2

Body Donation for Medical Education

Another option at the time of death is donating your body for medical education where your body will be used to teach medical students. This is to learn and help with overall training and to do things like:

- Teach anatomy.
- For very specific teaching and training.
- Or, research projects.

At the time of death, your next of kin would need to contact the school. Once released to the school, and after the school has completed the projects for which the body was assigned to, it is then followed by cremation. Please note that bodies can be used for medical education for as little as weeks up to six years, depending on where you live.

It is particularly important to note here that at the time of death, the family decides if they want the cremated remains. Yes, the cremated remains. Therefore, if you know you do not want to be cremated, then the option to donate your body to a medical school would not be an option for you.

Leaving your family to figure this out during that devastating time can cause a lot of confusion and heartache. If your family decides they do not want the cremated remains back, the medical school every two years (depending on where you live) has a Memorial Service for all donors and their families and then all the cremated remains are buried in a common grave.

It is very important for the family to understand this, and it is highly recommended to have a Memorial Service at the time of death. This way, families can celebrate their loved one and grieve together. A possibility of waiting up to six years could be very unsettling for some loved ones.

Overall, clearly communicating your wishes with your immediate family and completing the necessary registrations where applicable will always prevent delay and confusion at the time of death, keeping in mind that your next of kin will make the final decision. In both cases, even if one is registered for organ and tissue donation or body donation, there is a questionnaire that needs to be answered at the time of the call.

The body donation questionnaire over the phone is short, while the organ and tissue donation questionnaire is extensive and intrusive and can last up to 30 minutes or more. Some family members find that process very, very, difficult.

Not only are they being asked medical questions, but also travel questions, etc, so preparing them in advance will make the experience a little easier. Having a backup plan and advising your immediate family regarding next options if your organs, tissues, or body cannot be donated will mitigate possible confusion, chaos, and heartache during that time.

**Refer to Workbook Page(s):
Organ and Tissue Donation
or Body Used for Science
Page: 200**

92

Chapter 8

Senior Care

When you are no longer able to live on your own, where would you live?

Is your home set up to accommodate your special needs as you age?

If you lose mental capacity, who will take care of you?

Not only is dying a guaranteed part of life, but so is ageing. Having a plan in place before a crisis is not only easy on the senior but on the family and caregiver on a whole. Some adult children have not taken into consideration that their parents will get old and will need their help. Children will need to step up to be caregivers of their parents or have a plan in place to ensure their parent/parents are taken care of. Starting to have the conversations early before a possible crisis will alleviate having ageing parents turn on you because they are feeling like you are not on their side, or you are the enemy.

Referencing the Wills and Living Wills Chapter, if one loses mental capacity and none of the legal documents are set up, trying to get this done may result in a crisis which could make the process stressful for everyone. Remembering to ensure these documents are set up in advance is imperative.

Chapter 8:1

Family Caregivers Filing System

Starting a filing system with many file tabs per parent will save you a lot of stress, especially if there is an emergency. This way finding things is quick and easy. According to author Lorrie Morales, some of the file tabs mentioned in her book: *"We Can Do This: Adult Children and Ageing Parents Planning for Success"* could be:

- Medical history and medications
- Legal Documents (e.g., Wills)
- Passport
- Birth/marriage/divorce/adoption certificates
- Credit Card
- PIN numbers for accounts
- Bills (cable TV, telephone, power, water, taxes, gas)
- Vehicle information and insurance
- Mortgage or Rental Agreement
- Passwords for email, credit cards, debit card, accounts

Personally, I started the conversation with our parents after I realized the importance of having the conversation before a crisis and received a lot of push back regarding them having to move out of their home. At first, they did not agree with me at all, but as they are ageing, they are realizing that the three flights of stairs are no longer as easy to navigate as they were before. The thought of having the conversation in a crisis is very unsettling.

Having our parents disagree and be forced out of their home due to unexpected circumstances would only be harder on them and everyone else. Now they understand it, and when the time comes it will hopefully be a smoother transition for them, my siblings, and myself.

Chapter 8:2

Homecare Options for Seniors

Researching various Homecare options is one of the things that can be done in advance. Options may include setting up their own home to accommodate what is needed and ensuring that all safety measures have been considered is a good start.

In most cases, seniors do not want to leave their home, therefore, setting up safety measures like railings or ramps are just the start of many options. Researching various homecare options like having someone living in full time or part time or just having homecare help come in two or three times a day are also options for seniors to stay home.

Then there is the alternative to move into an ideal senior's home that would suit all their needs. There are so many options out there, therefore, doing the research and making a list of your top choices will likely mitigate having to settle with a less preferably or even unwanted location due to a crisis. Asking as many questions as possible and remembering to review the contract with an understanding of the fine print will save one from having to move their ageing parents from time to time.

For more information on Senior Care and knowing how to prepare for your ageing parents in advance, I recommend reading a book by Lorraine Lorrie Morales titled *"We Can Do This! Adult Children with Aging Parents Plan For Success."*

This book can be ordered from: "http://www.lorriemorales.com."

Chapter 9

Digital Legacy

Does your cell phone require a password for access?

Does your laptop or desktop need a password to gain access?

This is an often-neglected part of our personal lives – including myself. At the time of this writing, passwords for my hardware were neither known to my family nor written down somewhere easily accessible to them should I lose mental capacity or die. Hardware would be things like cell phones, laptops, desktops, iPads. etc. These devices store information that may be invaluable to our family or business partners now, however; access to the information stored on these devices will be critically important for our future decision makers to perform in their role as Power of Attorney, if one loses mental capacity, or as an Executor, at the time of death, with even a slight bit of success.

As Christine Brunsden said to me, it is like those left behind having to become professional hackers and/or detectives to try to gain access to these devices and the information contained within them during what is likely a devastating time for them. For example, when one dies, a loved one cannot go to the cell phone company to get the password to gain access to the phone. If your Executor does not have the password for your cell phone at the time of death, they will only be able to answer the phone and will have absolutely no way of getting into it. In many cases, they may never gain access to the device as providers are bound by privacy laws. Letting your loved ones know or writing down your passwords to your hardware would make things so much easier for them.

Amazingly, as of December 2021, Apple has recently announced their new legacy contact feature for all Apple users from IOS 15.2, iPadOS 15.2, and macOS 12.1. This feature allows the Apple user to set up a legacy contact for their device which gets activated when they pass away, allowing their contact to gain access to certain types of data from their Apple account. This is only accessible after they pass away.

This is a long, long time coming and finally, these companies are listening to the voices of devastated family members or more families are coming forward. I am confident that more and more digital companies will be doing the same in years to come.

I know this can get very messy. I heard of a situation whereby someone died in an accident and his phone was given to his wife by the police officer and that was how she found out that her husband was cheating on her for many years. Times like these, I am sure one would wish they did not have access to the phone. Situations like these make grieving so much more difficult. It is good practice to write down important telephone numbers and other useful information. A section at the back of this book is devoted to writing down your logins, letting your loved ones know where to find passwords and important telephone numbers. Remember that the best practice is to securely store your passwords separate from the inventory of your devices and other digital assets.

I know the next question is going to be about passwords for social media, bank accounts, etc. This is where it gets more complicated because it falls under Privacy Law & Estate Law which don't intersect well. Entering someone's bank accounts using their password could be a criminal offence as it falls under impersonation. During your lifetime, if you experience a loss in your account and you kept your login together with the password, the terms, and conditions you enter into with most banks do not normally provide for you to be compensated for the loss, if someone commits fraud using your information.

Remember the terms and conditions you read through fully when you loaded an app or set up a social media account (91% of us don't read them), they almost certainly prohibited the sharing of your password.

I am sure most of us would not want to see family members prosecuted for trying to locate the information they require to help make their job easier. There is a story of a lawsuit where parents got sued for getting into their son's Facebook account after his death. It really baffles me how being forced to get information can ultimately lead to being prosecuted if there is no permission or directive from the deceased. Trust me, I am still trying to figure out how it happened to those parents!

Things easily get complicated as many social media handles have little or no provisions for an Exit Plan when one dies. There is no contract or anything that is signed which expresses what to do when there is a death and whether to allow the account to be memorialised or deleted entirely. Your estate planning documents such as Powers of Attorney and Wills should have clauses that allow your decision makers to deal with your digital assets. Many people end up having to obtain court orders to deal with digital assets and often they have to obtain Orders in different countries if they live outside of the U.S.A because most social media platforms are headquartered in Southern California.

Unsurprisingly, death is one of those things that is not well talked about or researched with a clear direction for family, which creates confusion for everyone.

Chapter 9:1

Facebook Legacy Contact

For Facebook, there is a Legacy Contact setting which allows you to designate someone and lets them know to either memorialise or delete the account entirely. It gives them permission to do things like:

- Manage tribute posts
- Request the removal of an account
- Update pictures etc.

To access this on Facebook go to:

1. Settings & Privacy
2. Settings
3. General/Account Settings
4. Memorialization Settings

Please note that this way of accessing Facebook Legacy Contact might change in years to come.

For all your social media accounts, look to see if there is something like this that you can set up in advance.

When it comes to passwords for all other accounts like bank accounts, bills, subscriptions etc., all of those should not be accessed when one passes away and should be dealt with by the decision makers using their powers within the Estate Planning documents under which they were named.

Unless it is a joint account, there should be no one trying to gain access into these accounts. For more information on this, it is advisable to speak with a Wills and Estates Lawyer in your jurisdiction. It is important to have a digital inventory of things like this that will help those left behind and give them directions and permission on what to do.

Christine Brunsden, who lives in Burlington, Ontario, Canada, owns a company called Trusted Legacy; she has built a digital asset inventory that can help you organise your affairs and provide a blueprint for your future decision makers.

Go to www.trustedlegacy.ca for more information. Or, look up other companies that have a digital inventory that can help put a plan in place for all digital assets today.

**Refer to Workbook Page(s):
Hardware Login Information
Pages: 225-226**

Chapter 10

Updating Documents on a Regular Basis

How often do you update important personal documents or records?

Quarterly? Annually? Or rarely?

Life happens and it is so easy to forget to update our paperwork with all our important and recent information. There could be changes in our marital status, beneficiaries, investments, and overall health. Our important documents could be related to insurance, property, finances, and real estate. In fact, it is advisable to discuss and review all these important documents before living together or getting married and signing the Registration of Marriage form.

Have you ever heard of a situation where a couple gets married and say for example the wife moves into the husband's home?

Let's say, unfortunately years later, the husband passes away and the wife is asked to move out of their home, only now does the wife find out that the house was not solely owned by her deceased husband but was jointly owned with his brother. When two people own a home, and the ownership on the title shows "joint tenants," when one dies, the surviving tenant automatically gets full ownership of the home.

Situations like this are very unfortunate, especially when the spouse who moved in had her own property and sold it and did not ask the right questions. Unfortunately, with a situation like this, the brother has the right to evict his sister-in-law from his property. Ways to avoid a situation like this is possibly asking to see the title or deed on the home to verify ownership before assuming it to be marital property.

Another unfortunate surprise is when someone dies and none of the important paperwork is changed to reflect updated beneficiaries. Could you imagine your spouse passing away and the beneficiaries listed on their personal insurance products or work benefits have not been updated? What if the listed beneficiary happens to be an ex-spouse?

Work benefits documentation is filled out in the first couple of days when starting a new job. Imagine a situation where one completes this paperwork on the very first day of work and stays at the same company for over 40 years and in that 40-year period, they have remarried twice. How easy is it to forget to go back to their Human Resources Department to update their beneficiaries on file? Once again, it can be a very unfortunate surprise.

Oh my! I almost forgot to mention another common scenario. How about a situation where one is separated for a very long time, and does not actually legally divorce his or her spouse? If one dies, their pension could end up going to their 'estranged' spouse. This especially gets difficult when there are minor children involved, and the pension was a private pension that could have been set up for the children. Pensions can get very complicated, depending on the type, but the question is, if you had taken the time to think about it in advance, would you have avoided getting that divorce if you knew the pension would end up going to your ex-spouse instead of your children? As stated above, although pensions are complicated, you are the best person to determine the best beneficiary for your pension.

Not having a plan in place and not remembering to update and review important paperwork, could result in missed opportunities for disappointed beneficiaries. An accidental omission can be costly. The more we realise how important it is to ensure updates and reviews are done regularly, the less chance there is for unexpected surprises during a devastating time.

Chapter 10:1

Significant Milestones to Update Documents

Here in Canada, our personal taxes are due in April every year. Perhaps using tax time as a reminder to review and update your documents yearly is a good practice. If you get into the habit of updating other important documents during the tax season each year and during any significant milestones in your life, such as:

- Birth of a child.

- Death in the family.

- Before marriage.

- Marital or relationship breakdown.

- Death of an Executor, Trustee, Guardian, Attorney (under a Power of Attorney) or Agent.

- Relocation of Executor outside of your province/state or country.

- Change in your assets or liabilities.

There would be much less of an opportunity for things to go wrong at the time of a death.

Happy updating your important documents!!!

Refer to Workbook Page(s):
Emergency Contact Details
Page: 203

Family & Friends Contact Details
Pages: 204 - 211

Important Documents Log
Pages: 214 - 224

Chapter 11

Taxes

Do you know your estate could be taxed on death?

Do you know the tax implications on your assets?

Do you know what assets should be put through your estate so that the tax bill is equal amongst your beneficiaries?

Death and taxes are a few of the most guaranteed things in life. As much as we do not want to discuss death or deal with our taxes, there are definite repercussions when we ignore either of these topics. As a matter of fact, the issues with taxes vary and it depends on where you live and how the tax laws will be applied when one dies. Doing research in advance before distributing assets will give a better idea of what assets will be taxed more than others so that they are distributed fairly.

Depending where one lives, the tax on death can be calculated on the gross fair market value of one's assets, well, that depends on the asset, because not all assets are taxable. The tax on death is due to be paid by a certain time from the time of death, for example, it could be six months from the date of a death. The tax rate amount, for example, could be 18%-40% depending on where one lives.

What assets could attract taxes? They include things like:

- Assets in your name like stocks, bonds, and bank accounts.

- Real estate, retirement assets.

- In Canada, principal residence is exempt from tax, along with some household furnishings and personal items.

Keep in mind that in some cases, the value of property owned jointly with a spouse may also be included in the calculations.

Following up with an accountant in your jurisdiction will give you a better idea as to what the tax obligation would be. Additionally, in Canada, assets that are transferred to a married spouse or common-law partner upon a death, are afforded a tax deferral until the death of the surviving spouse or common-law partner, unless you elect out of this spousal rollover.

An example of an unfair distribution, in Canada, would be leaving one child as the beneficiary of your registered retirement accounts, and then leaving your estate to your other child. One child could end up with more money because of how the distribution was structured, and the other child is left bearing the burden of the taxes in the estate.

It is one thing to lose a loved one but add in all the various surprises that come up afterwards, such as a large tax bill, and it can seem all too overwhelming. It is crucial to avoid an unintentional and unfair distribution of your hard-earned assets and prevent possible family disputes. This can easily be planned for and avoided by getting professional help and proper legal and tax advice ahead of time.

Chapter 12

Prepaid Funeral Home and Cemetery Packages

Does your family know what you want when you pass away?

Did you know that you could pay the funeral home and cemetery bill well in advance with a lump sum or payment plan?

How prepared will your family be to make permanent decisions in the midst of grief?

Pre-planning your final disposition wishes at the funeral home directly, or with a Pre-planning Specialist like myself, who has a working relationship with funeral homes, is the process of drafting up your plans for your final disposition wishes. This is for a funeral, memorial, direct burial, or cremation in advance before the service is needed. Opening a file with information that will be needed when one passes away is included.

Doing this in advance will help your family immensely in the first 24 hours when they are going through shock and there is a lot of confusion on what to do. Because there are so many decisions to be made when going to the funeral home at the time of a passing, putting a plan in place will also protect families from having to make permanent decisions in a short time.

Chapter 12:1

Benefits of Prepaid Pre-Arrangements

There are several benefits for setting up your prepaid pre-arrangements at a funeral home or cemetery today.

These include:

Funeral Home:

- Paid for and locked in at today's dollars and guarantees the price at the funeral home.

- Your final disposition wishes will be honoured and will not be someone else's wishes.

- Various payment plan options to fit in your budget.

- Paid out directly to the funeral home at the time of death.

- Takes away the potential of family breakdowns due to disagreements.

- No overspending due to emotional spending at the time of a death.

- Loved ones can just grief and be in the moment and not have to worry.

Cemetery:

- Lock in today's dollars and guarantee the price.

- Purchase family plots in advance so family can be together.

- Understand the differences between the cemeteries so you can make an informed decision (ex. public, private, religious).

Setting up your prepaid pre-arrangement at the funeral home can be as basic or as specific as possible. This can be as simple as just paying for your casket/urn or taking care of everything including flowers and the catering bills. It is completely up to you and what you are comfortable doing.

Chapter 12:2

Payment Options

Your payment/non-payment options are:

- Pay a lump sum.

- Set up a monthly payment plan.

- Set up a file at the funeral home where your final disposition wishes are kept along with other important information (no payment necessary).

If you opt for the monthly payment plan, it is a pre-need group insurance policy created specifically for funeral homes. This is designed to look after the funds until a death has occurred.

(**Please note:** Prices are locked in and guaranteed by the funeral home. Third-party expenses such as catering are not guaranteed but money can be put aside for that expense that can be put towards that bill at the time of a death.)

For example, in Canada, Assurant Life of Canada/TruStage Life of Canada is the funeral funder for 95% of the funeral homes in Canada. When a pre-arrangement program is set up with a payment plan or lump-sum, Assurant Life of Canada/TruStage Life of Canada holds the funds.

This means that the money can be transferable to another funeral home if needed.

Paperwork for the funeral home and Assurant Life/TruStage Life of Canada is done together and is held at the funeral home of choice, Assurant Life of Canada/TruStage Life of Canada and you, the policyholder. This combines both the funding and the file with final arrangements at the funeral home.

If you do not want to start paying in advance for a pre-arrangement package, a good first step is going to a funeral home and opening a file so they can start collecting your information and documenting your final disposition wishes.

Don't forget to ask for a quote or pricing for the funeral home of choice. I am confident that once you look at the pricing years later, you will see a price increase the next time you go visit the funeral home. This is due to inflation costs as funeral home prices go up a minimum of once a year.

Chapter 12:3

Cremation Guaranteed

Setting up your prepaid pre-arrangements is important if you want to be cremated. This is especially important if the public trustee gets involved with your final disposition arrangements. A public trustee is assigned when there is no one to help with the final arrangements at the funeral home or when there is no money to take care of the funeral home bill. At times, there is no Executor, family, or friends to help with the final arrangements.

If you want to be cremated and it is stated in your Will, that is not enough if the public trustee gets involved. Depending on where you live, if the public trustee gets involved and you have your prepaid arrangements set up, whether it is in your Will or not, your wishes will be granted. If your Will states that you want to be cremated and you did not leave money to pay for your cremation through a pre-arrangement at a Funeral Home and the Public Trustee gets involved, they will opt for the most cost-effective burial package. One of the reasons for this is that someone needs to sign off for cremation. For example, if a family member comes forward years later and wants access to your remains, a cremation cannot be undone. Someone will need to be held accountable for that decision and the Public Trustee will not.

Whether it is the funeral home bill or the cemetery bill, they are both bills that need to be taken care of soon after the time of a passing or before the Celebration of Life. One of the biggest advantages of preplanning and paying in advance, the funeral home or cemetery bill is locked in and guarantees today's dollars.

For example, I know of a close family friend who bought her plot in Calgary back in the 80's for just under $600.00 and now that same plot value today September 25, 2021, is worth over $5,000.00. If grandma did not pre-pay her cemetery bill in advance, the cemetery bill would have been over $5,000.00 when she died.

When a family member goes to the funeral home or cemetery and realises that both financial and non-financial decisions were made in advance, it takes away a lot of the stress and brings peace of mind. This allows them to just grieve which also leaves a positive legacy. Keep in mind that someone will need to cover the cost of the funeral home bill until insurance is figured out, and that is if there is insurance or money set aside to cover the bill.

Some funeral homes will wait for the insurance to pay the bill, but it depends on the funeral home. Having a prepaid pre-arrangement will take away that burden on loved ones during that devastating time.

Not only does pre-paying the funeral home bill and cemetery bill in advance save money but it also takes away the:

- Chaos
- Confusion
- Possible family breakdown

Remember, managing the business of dying now will ensure that your wishes are granted and will leave your family with clarity and comfort to make fewer decisions at the time of your passing, so they can just grieve.

Chapter 12:4

Low-Cost Repatriation Benefit

Repatriation is the return of a loved one to their own country when they pass away.

This is also a product that can be obtained when setting up a prepaid funeral home package. Repatriation involves two funeral homes, one at the place of death to prepare the deceased before going home and the other is wherever home is. Setting up your prepaid packages or setting up a file at the funeral home where your final wishes are kept will help your family immensely.

Losing a loved one is one thing but losing a loved one while they are on vacation, for example, is another. No words can explain how such an unpleasant task it is to bring a loved one home following a death. Death is so unpredictable, so setting up a repatriation protection and hoping it will not be needed is another great gift for loved ones.

(**Please note,** this protection brings you home to your primary place of residence. For example, if on vacation, it will return you home to your primary residence. But, if you live and pass away in Greece and you want to be returned to Canada, this is not covered because your primary residence is in Greece.)

Putting a plan in place today will make the first 24-48 hours easier for families. This will bring peace of mind and will give them an opportunity to just grieve and be in the moment following the days after a loved one's passing.

**Refer to Workbook Page(s):
Vital Statistics
Pages: 227-228**

**Funeral Home & Cemetery Instructions
Pages: 229-232**

Chapter 13

Funeral Homes and Cemeteries

Do you know which funeral home to call if a loved one passes away?

Have you ever visited a funeral home or cemetery for information gathering?

Did you know that the funeral home is separate from the cemetery?

The first question that is asked when a loved one passes away is, "What funeral home would you like us to contact to care for your loved one"?

Such a question is one of the most difficult things to hear once a loved one passes away. Nevertheless, the question will have to be answered right away depending on whether the hospital/hospice/homecare has the facility or capacity to keep the loved one while deciding. When one passes away, it is a hard reality when the hospital/homecare can no longer help your loved one and they no longer belong at that facility. Depending on where you live, the family may have to decide on which funeral home will be notified to take care of your loved one right away.

Chapter 13:1

Funeral Homes

Types of funeral homes (depending on where you live):

- Family run
- Private
- Corporate

Funeral homes offer varying services. Some are full service funeral homes which provide a complete range of services and there are the low-cost alternatives which may have fewer services available. For example, they may only offer the option for cremation and not burial services.

Choosing a funeral home, visiting them, and getting pricing is not a hard task once you know your final wishes and know what is important to you. If you do not have a funeral home in mind, start by asking others whose families have used a funeral home, reaching out to a church or a community association and asking them their opinions. Going to visit the funeral home or speaking with a Pre-Planning Specialist like myself will save loved ones from making a decision in a crisis.

Things to consider while choosing a particular funeral home:

- Proximity.

- How accommodating is the funeral home?

- Appearance of the facility.

- Are they so busy that you are more considered a number as opposed to someone who lost a loved one?

- Do they have a great reputation?

- Are the employees compassionate and understanding?

- Do they understand your cultural or religious values and customs?

- Do they have experience working with your community?

- Are they family run or corporate? For those who support local businesses.

- Do they have affordable packages?

If affordability is important to you, getting two or three quotes from different funeral homes is a great way to understand what is affordable for your family.

Guess why some families overpay at the time of death? The number one reason is that no research was done in advance or there were no prepaid pre-arrangements set up at a funeral home to lock in or guarantee the rates. Once you know what is important to you, choosing a funeral home in advance at times will make your family's experience a more favourable one at the time of a passing.

Chapter 13:2

Cemeteries

If you wish to be buried at a cemetery, heading to a cemetery is the next step after going to a funeral home at the time of a passing. Whether the funeral home has a cemetery attached or not, the funeral home side of this process is separate, resulting in families speaking with two separate entities. For clarity, the funeral home is where a loved one is taken from the time of death to be cared for and the cemetery is the final resting place.

The primary purpose of the cemetery is the dignified disposition of human remains, according to provincial and municipal laws. The cemetery is the place where human remains or ashes are buried.

Types of Cemeteries

Depending on your city, province/state, and country, there are various cemeteries to choose from, typically they are:

- Public
- Private
- Religious

There are pros and cons to each of them so doing research in advance before a death occurs will help with making a wise decision. Below is a brief comparison of public and private cemeteries in Calgary, Alberta. This brief comparison will help one to understand why it is important to do research in advance.

Public

- Publicly run.

- Do not need a burial vault (an outer container that encloses a casket).

- Do not have to put on a headstone.

- Cannot do a payment plan to purchase a plot in advance

- Must pay a lump sum when purchasing in advance.

- More cost effective.

- Cemetery will buy back the plot at today's value up to a percentage and the plot cannot be sold privately. (The city will buy back the plot).

Private

- Burial vaults are required (an outer container that encloses a casket).

- Recommended to have the headstone installed by the 1st year after the death.

- Arrange a monthly payment plan or pay a lump sum in full.

- Much higher cost.

- Cemetery will buy back the plot up to a percentage of what it was bought for, or it can be sold privately.

Things to keep in mind when deciding on cemetery selections are:

- Size of the plots - How many caskets or urns can fit in the plot (e.g.: double depth fitting two caskets).

- Whether or not a family plot is available?

- Opening and closing fees - Amount to dig open and close the plot at the time of a death.

- Headstones - If there is a minimum size or type of stone required (this can make a difference on the total cost).

- Weekend or Long Weekend Rates - If there is a service on a weekend, there will, or there could incur additional costs (e.g., Sundays or on a long weekend, fees can double or triple depending on the cemetery fees).

Understanding the differences between available options in your jurisdiction and knowing that each cemetery has their own guidelines and regulations will help with making a wise decision for families.

**Refer to Workbook Page(s):
Funeral Home & Cemetery Instructions
Pages: 229-232**

Chapter 14

End-of-Life Doula and Death Café

Have you heard of a Death Café or an End-of-Life Doula before?

Working in the Death and Dying Industry, I have had to embrace continuous learning that I can share with others. I first learned about End-of-Life Doulas also known as Death Doulas and Death Cafes in September 2019. We were running seminars in Kelowna, BC, Canada when I met two End-of-Life Doulas who attended one of the seminars and my first thought was, 'what did I get myself into'? I had never heard of that term before. Instantly, I became curious and wanted to learn more about End-of-Life Doulas in case anyone ever asked me about it. After speaking with them, I was then invited to a Death Café.

By that time, I was once again asking myself the question: "What am I doing in this Industry?"

Even though I had plans to return home by a certain time and date, I knew I had to change my plans in order to attend and learn more about the Death Café. But here's the funny part, friends and family seemed more nervous than I was, remaining in Kelowna to check out the Death Café, especially after I sent them the invite for the event.

Chapter 14.1

Death Café

I guess by now, you are wondering what is a Death Café? It is a FREE event with no agenda and a safe place to have discussions about death. A Death Café is an International Organisation founded by John Underwood in 2011. These Cafes are held all over the world, and it should be easy to find one in your area or close by.

One of the positive things about Death Cafes since the pandemic is that most of these are now run online, so it opens more opportunities to visit various cafes irrespective of where you reside. As you know, the subject of death is not easily discussed so attending one of these cafes would be a great place to learn and speak to others who are comfortable with talking about death.

These groups help to break the ice, especially talking with family members about the topic of death. The more dialogue held about death gives us the opportunity to think about the process and plan for the future.

Chapter 14:2

End of Life Doula (Death Doula)

What exactly is an End-of-Life Doula and how does it differ from a Death Café? An End-of-Life Doula is a non-medical professional trained to care for a terminally ill person's physical, emotional, spiritual, and holistic needs during the death process. They typically work along with hospice or End-of-Life Care Staff providing support and care for those in the last phase of a life-limiting illness. They recognize dying as a part of the normal process of living and help families understand that as well.

Their main focus is on the quality of life for individuals and family caregivers. They offer support to the family and assist the family during the death process. Not only do they support the family but also the person who is dying. I refer to them like a coach who understands what is happening and makes the death process easier on the terminally ill person and their family.

If you choose to use an End-of-Life Doula in your area, I recommend you interview two or three of them, review their websites, assess their personality and even spirituality. Choosing an End-of-Life Doula who does not share similar values and beliefs with you could lead to an unintended negative outcome. Losing a loved one is a very vulnerable time for everyone, so it is important to research the right

End-of-Life Doula and take the time to set expectations and communicate what is important to you.

End-of-Life Doulas are not fully accepted everywhere in the world, but they definitely bring a different skill set and education to society, especially for those who are fully prepared to go through the process of dealing with death. Their inspiration in this phase of life is needed because the reality of death can be beautiful, difficult, ugly, surprising, short, or a long process, etc., depending on the level of preparation or the lack thereof. We need someone who understands and can hold the space for our families especially because death traumatises some family members. The more we learn about what death looks like before it happens from professionals in the Death and Dying Industry, the easier it will be for everyone.

I recently was helping with a Celebration of Life Service and one of the grandson's said that death is beautiful. He was one of the grandchildren who was blessed to spend the most time with their grandad before his passing. Could you imagine if more and more people had that experience and how some of our thoughts on death could change the world?

Yes, death anxiety and death trauma are real – planting those seeds well in advance through talking more about death and pre-planning for death would make families experiences less traumatizing.

For more information on Death Doulas near you or Death Doula training:

In Canada, go to:

https://ddnbc.com/

or

https://endoflifedoulaassociation.org/

In USA, go to:

https://www.internationaldoulalifemovement.com/directory

or

https://www.nedalliance.org/end-of-life_doulas_a_through_m.html

Chapter 15

Grief

What is Grief?

Did you know that if your affairs are not in order before death, there could be compounded grief experienced by your family?

Have you ever uttered the words 'Be Strong' to someone who is grieving?

If guilt was not an issue, would grief be as difficult, or would it be easier?

Grief is a natural response to loss. It is the emotional suffering one feels when something or someone they love is taken away. In some cases, the loss can be overwhelming, unbearable to the point of it being paralysing and debilitating to one's life.

Grief is a multitude of emotions including, however not limited to, shock, sadness, anger, shame, and guilt, amongst other feelings.

Grief is a journey and an ongoing process. Unfortunately, grief does not leave us, however, we simply learn to adjust and adapt daily. Being patient with oneself and coming to terms with the reality of the loss, will help alleviate the intensity of the pain. Experiencing loss in our lifetime is a normal occurrence in life, we all will encounter.

Chapter 15:1

Ways To Alleviate Stress Before A Passing

Getting one's affairs in order can help to alleviate the stress that can add to the grief loved ones experience, and oftentimes it may prevent them from commencing their grieving process. The grief of losing a loved one intensifies when it is coupled with difficulties when a loved one did not have their affairs in order before their passing.

Therefore, not avoiding the crucial conversations about death, your final wishes, financial cost, pre-planning may be the greatest gift one can leave for their loved ones. The choices made today can make life easier and/or be a seamless process for those who remain when a loved one passes away.

So, how do we alleviate the whole gamut of guilt, stress, worry, fear, anxiety, conflict, etc. that may occur when a loved one passes away? Some ways of alleviating these at the time of death include:

- Having the uncomfortable conversation as soon as possible.

- Expressing what your final wishes are which removes the guesswork at the time of a death.

- Have your financial affairs in place.

- Being honest and letting family know if you are terminally ill and giving them an opportunity to spend time with you (I know, this is a difficult one).

- Watch our words, respect, and treat people with kindness, and demonstrate love always.

- Live life as though it were your last day on earth.

- Forgive others and make peace. Time is not guaranteed, use it wisely.

Have you ever said to someone who is grieving, "Be strong and do not cry"? I remember the days I used to tell people to be strong and to not cry. Now I question myself, wondering why and where did I learn that supporting method.

Losing a loved one is one of the worst experiences anyone will ever go through and there is no reason on earth why one should not cry. Why in that moment exercise strength or be strong? Be strong for whom? I can't exactly say for yourself, because not crying and not going through the grieving process will only worsen it for us, our family and those around us.

Chapter 15:2

Grief Support

While everyone's grief journey is different, I personally think that grief is something that we cannot work through on our own. Finding a grief coach/counsellor, reading books, talking to someone who has been through it and understands our situation will be a great help to us throughout this journey. Grief coaches are similar to that of our sports coaches when we were in school. Our sports coach taught us how to be the best player by giving us advice and tips on how to navigate the sport to be a star. This is similar to having a grief coach who we could collaborate with to give us tips that will guide us through the grief journey.

Once we come to the realization that we are not doing well and need help, reaching out for support will save us a lot of sleepless nights, and help provide relief from guilt, stress, fear, and suffering in general.

Researching various coaches/counsellors, grief support groups in your area or government funded support groups will help you on the journey of grief. Please do not go on this journey alone and know there is a lot of support out there. You just have to be honest with yourself and ask for support.

Chapter 16

Bucket List and Creating Memories

Do you have a Bucket list?

Did you know that the memories that are created with loved ones today are the memories that will bring them the most comfort after losing a loved one?

A Bucket list is several experiences or achievements that a person hopes to have or accomplish during their lifetime. Yes, this is before we "kick-the-bucket."

Having a bucket list and setting deadlines is so important, especially as it is very evident all around the world how fragile life is. Even though we all dream and hope to live through our youth, spend precious moments with our children and/or grandchildren and enjoy our retirement, the reality is that we have no clue when our last day on earth will be because tomorrow is not guaranteed.

I was asked this question recently," if you knew that you had one week left to live, what would you do"? One of my thoughts was that I needed to hurry up and get this book done, amongst other answers.

I now know that being more purposeful means more to me than ever before. There is a saying that says "The graveyard is the richest place on Earth" because it is a place where one will find numerous unfulfilled hopes and dreams. The books that were never written, the songs that were never sung, the inventions that were never shared, the cures that were never discovered, all because someone was afraid to fully share their talent with the world or thought they had all the time in the world to pursue those dreams.

Working on our bucket list, creating beautiful and lasting memories with our family and friends, contributes to dying with a peace of mind. The worst thing is being on our deathbed, self-reflecting and being hit with the reality that we no longer have the opportunity to accomplish more in life could bring immense regret.

The most rewarding bonus is creating lasting memories with our family and friends so those memories will be memories that will bring comfort and peace of mind to family and friends after one passes away.

Remember to live your best life today because tomorrow is not promised.

**Refer to Workbook Page(s):
My Bucket List
Pages: 255-258**

Chapter 17

Pictures/Obituary/Eulogy/ Record a Song/Letter Writing

"Ladies and gentlemen, as we start our descent, please put your seat backs and tray tables in their full upright position. Make sure your seat belt is securely fastened and all carry-on luggage is stowed underneath the seat in front of you or in the overhead bins. Thank you."

"Flight attendants, prepare for landing please."
"Cabin crew, please take your seats for landing."

Do your children or spouse know your family tree for your Eulogy?

Should your ex-spouse or stepchildren be on the video tribute at your Celebration of Life?

Do you have specific pictures that you would like shown at your Celebration of Life?

Organizing a Celebration of Life Service can at times be incredibly stressful for loved ones at the time of death, not to mention thinking of ways to notify friends and the community. The more things that can be arranged beforehand, the more it will help loved ones during this difficult time and allow them the opportunity to just grieve. Remember, planning ahead does not mean you are going to die, it is an act of love and shows consideration of how difficult it will be for your family to be at peace during such a painful time in their life. It will also have them talking and sharing about such a beautiful gift that was left to other family and friends for years and years to come.

Chapter 17:1

Pictures

Going through pictures and finding pictures to be used for the video tribute at the Celebration of Life Service can be emotionally draining yet therapeutic at the same time. But the hardest part is trying to find the pictures and figuring out who is who in each picture at times.

The question here is, how can one start to put pictures aside and organizing pictures in advance. One suggestion is to start to write names and dates at the back of pictures that one already has. I know, I am sure some people are wondering, why would I start to do that. Believe it or not, this idea has brought many people peace of mind, especially those who are planners and would like to put as many things in order to help their loved ones.

How about digital pictures? An idea for this is to create a folder on your desktop, laptop or i-Pad/tablet and start putting pictures in the folder. No, you do not have to label it "Pictures To Use When I Die", it can just say something like, "My Pictures." And for those who are very detail-oriented, they can also save the picture with the names of the people in the picture and the year it was taken; this can also include labelling the cover picture for the program.

In that same folder, you can add a word document with as little or as much detail as you like to help explain those pictures.

Let those memories begin!!

Chapter 17:2

Obituary

An Obituary is an announcement of a death in the newspaper or other media along with the biography of the deceased.

This is optional and, in more cases, than before, families opt out of this option. We find that more families are opting to use the funeral homes website for this announcement instead. Because so many people are on social media and less and less people are using newspapers, seniors are more likely to stick to this option for now. I do not know; this might be one of those things that might just fade away one day but only time will tell.

Chapter 17:3

Eulogy

A Eulogy is a speech or piece of writing that is presented at the Celebration of Life Service. This writing gives a biography of the deceased along with sharing a synopsis of their life and praising them. The absence of a pre-planned Obituary and Eulogy places extra burden on our loved ones to prepare and determine what aspects must be shared. This is in addition to the many decisions that must be made during this devastating time. Having the discussion in advance or even writing down important names and information will help your loved ones put this together without offending anyone or getting wrong information.

I recently attended a Celebration of Life Service where there was no Eulogy. It left me wondering if the family did not have this information or maybe there was some disagreement among family members or that they simply forgot such an important part of the service. Quite frankly, it is possible for things to get mixed up or missed during a Celebration of Life Service when working under such stress.

I will even take it a step further, what about when there is a mixed family? Is it right or wrong to include the following to the Eulogy?:

- Ex's when there are children involved.
- Ex's who are deceased.
- Multiple exes.
- Stepchildren.
- Estranged children, (i.e.: limited or broken relationship).

This can get extensive and causes a lot of confusion and contention among family members when this is not discussed beforehand. The question I have is, "Is it fair for our families to be tasked with determining who gets honourable mentions and/or even yet, left to figure out a possible mess"?

Early discussions and pre-planning can reduce such risk and avoidable problems that can cause family breakdowns, incite tension, and cause divisions during an already difficult and stressful time.

Chapter 17:4

Record a Song

Could you imagine writing a song or having a pre-recorded song played at your Celebration of Life Service? This is another beautiful, memorable gift and such a welcoming surprise for family and friends to memorialize you.

Overall, preparing for the inevitable and putting something in place in advance brings peace of mind to loved ones. Recording a song would continually bring comfort to family and friends for years and years to come.

Chapter 17:5

Letter Writing/Recordings

Letter writing or leaving recordings is such a beautiful gift to loved ones when one passes away.

Pre-planning these memorable messages sooner rather than later ensures that it is available and ready for broadcast in the event of an unforeseen passing.

A few years ago, I watched a movie in which a mother passed away. Prior to her death, she wrote letters to her daughter for every milestone in her life. I remember thinking how beautiful that was and how doing that would mean the world to loved ones. From my experience, loved ones always look forward to some kind of connection or memories linked to the deceased. This will be amazing during a sudden passing especially if there was no time to say goodbye or the last opportunity to express how proud they are of their loved ones and much more. These messages help with the grieving process when such recordings or letters are addressed and shared with loved ones - something personal will let your loved ones know that they will be okay and how much they are cherished.

How about taking it a step further and making a video of oneself to be played at your Celebration of Life Service for your family and friends?

Refer to Workbook Page(s):
About Me
Pages: 233-240

Letters for My Loved Ones
Pages: 248-252

Chapter 18

Legacy

"Ladies and gentlemen, we have just been cleared to land. Please make sure one last time that your seat belt is securely fastened. The flight attendants are currently passing around the cabin to make a final compliance check and pick up any remaining cups and glasses. Thank you."

How do you want to be remembered?

What lessons do you hope to pass along to your children, grandchildren, and great grandchildren?

What do you think you would be known for after your passing?

Growing up, I always thought that Legacy meant a dollar value, in other words, a financial gift to give your family when you pass away. I often wondered why it had to be about money when there are so many other things that parents and loved ones can pass down to their family that are not connected to a dollar value. Much later, I learned that Legacy is about life and living it. It is about learning from the past, living in the present and building for the future. Not only is it not only about money but it is also about sharing love, having lived a life well lived, rather than just existing.

Overall, when one dies, the memorable mark that remains on those left behind would be their Legacy. Whether it is receiving proceeds from their estate, or the richness of a life well lived will determine one's Legacy. It also could depend on who they were, what was important to them and their values.

Have you ever thought about how you will be remembered by others when you pass away? Or, if the world would be a better place because of the contributions you made during your lifetime towards the betterment of society? Identifying what is important to you and demonstrating it throughout your lifetime speaks volumes, without the utterance of a word will have a long-lasting impact on the lives of those who remain. If one says that family is of utmost importance to them, and their family does not agree or feels the same, then it's safe to say that this would not be a part of one's Legacy.

A saying has it that "Your Legacy is the ultimate person you want to become."

Unfortunately, there are negative legacies just as there are positive legacies and if we are not careful, the negative Legacy is what will define us when we are no longer around. Not only does negative legacies ruin our character, it also can be very painful for others especially when a secret comes out after we are no longer around to defend or explain ourselves. The revelation of secret(s) held for many years is one of the most devastating things that contributes to the already difficult grieving process.

I can understand that at times we want to protect our loved ones, however, this results in causing more damage than actual protection. While I do not advocate that people start letting out all secrets, I highly recommend that people consider writing a letter or saving a video or voice recording to a loved one explaining the situation, why they did not tell them and that they are sorry. This would make a world of difference to our loved one's grief journey and our Legacy.

I recall in my youth hearing the saying that some secrets need to be taken to our grave. I do agree with the statement, especially when there is no possibility for that secret to be shared after one's passing. In my experience, just like some of us, I have witnessed many cases when one dies and all kinds of secrets are revealed. Therefore, for those who may have a secret and if it comes out after their passing, writing a letter, or having a voice or video message that is saved somewhere and noted in the Will; might be a suggestion. This will bring peace of mind to the person who is dying.

The thought of living one's last hours/days fearing the potential of a secret coming out could be very unsettling. This way, spending time with family can be top priority making lasting memories instead.

Chapter 18:1

Examples of Legacy

Overall, legacies can be simple or very extensive, however, the best part about your Legacy is it's your choice as to what your life story will be. This will also include what will be passed from one generation to the next.

This can be for example:

- Money or property.
- Accomplishments.
- Character (e.g.: how you treat people or how you handle situations).
- Adding value to those around you.
- Adding value to the place you work for a powerful Legacy.
- Being a mentor.
- Being a leader.
- Doing good deeds like volunteering.
- Passing your skills and knowledge to others.
- Knowing your mission and vision.

- Donating money.
- Showing love.
- Family traditions and family recipes.
- Sharing and telling your story.

This list can be extensive but just remember that Legacy is a long-time haul and does not happen overnight. Taking the time to think about what you want your Legacy to be like and being intentional about it and writing it down definitely helps one to leave a positive Legacy for generations to come.

As a Licensed Pre-planning Specialist, how can I not mention the act of love and putting a plan together for your final departure that will also bring your family peace of mind during that devastating time?

Leaving a positive Legacy and putting a plan in place is the final act of love towards those you are leaving behind. Holding their hand and guiding them through the most difficult time of their lives when they need you the most is a gift of love. Passing the Legacy of putting a plan in place so generations after generations can learn and see how important it is will help more families to experience the beauty of having a positive death experience.

"Legacy is about life and living. It's about learning from the past, living in the present and building for the future. Legacy is the ultimate person you become."

**Refer to Workbook Page(s):
My Legacy
Pages: 253-254**

Chapter 19

What to do with My Stuff

"Ladies and gentlemen, welcome to your Final Departure. For your safety and comfort, please remain seated with your seat belt fastened until the Captain turns off the Fasten Seat Belt sign. This will indicate that we have parked at the gate and that it is safe for you to move about. At this time, you may use your cellular phones if you wish. Cellular phones may only be used once the Fasten Seat Belt sign has been turned off.

Please check around your seat for any personal belongings you may have brought on board with you and please use caution when opening the overhead bins, as heavy articles may have shifted around during the flight.

If you require deplaning assistance, please remain in your seat until all other passengers have deplaned. One of our crew members will then be pleased to assist you."

If you were to put all your stuff in storage, how much room would you need?

Does your family know what to do with all your stuff when you are gone?

One of the least things that a person thinks about is "What should my family do with all my stuff when I am gone?" Year after year we continue to collect and buy items. Even though much of it means a lot to us, at times, it means nothing to someone else. We hear stories of individuals passing away and the family is rushed to move or get rid of some of their personal belongings. Dealing with such a devastating time and then getting rushed to move things causes families to either throw away items or even have strangers come and take things because there was no plan in place on what to do with all the stuff.

This can cause a lot of confusion, especially if it is ageing parents who have passed and their children have their own place and do not need anything. Or their children feeling that the things that mom or dad had are outdated and they do not want them.

Yes, in some cases stuff will be listed in the Will but what about the other stuff? Or if there is no Will and no direction on what to do?

Losing a loved one and all that comes with it is one thing, being in the midst of grief is yet another and to add the pressure of trying to organize, sell, clean, and oversee all personal belongings can be a very negative experience. These situations can push loved ones over the edge. To add another twist is when a family is out of town and must come into town to sort through all the stuff and figure out what to do in a short window of time.

Did you know there are companies families can call to help during these difficult times? These are Professional Organizers and Full-Service Estate Sale Companies who can come in and do the mental and physical work for your loved ones. They can do as little or as much that is needed to get this task complete. For some of the estate sales companies, there are no out-of-pocket expenses because they operate based on an agreed-upon percentage of the income from the sale of the stuff, for their fee. This depends on where you live and market rates out there.

They will do things like:

- Go through the house, room by room and sort things out with your loved one.

- Sort out stuff for charities (donation) and what to give to family and friends.

- Sort things in a memories bin to possibly go through at a later date.

- Sell stuff.

- Work with a team of appraisers to appraise various items.

- Sort through stuff to go in the dumpster.

- And more.

Marcy Norman, one of the Franchise Owners here in Calgary, AB of a Full-Service Estate Sales Company called Sell My Stuff Canada shared with me some of the above. Sell my Stuff Canada services Alberta, Ontario, and Quebec.

For more information, go to: www.sellmystuffcanada.com

For those who do not live in Canada, research professional organisers or Full-Service Estate Sales Companies for a listing near you. This is another great way to bring peace of mind to loved ones during a devastating time.

**Refer to Workbook Page(s):
What To Do With My Stuff
Pages: 259 - 261**

Chapter 20

Challenge

How do you manage surprises in a crisis?

Would you rather get more information in advance before a death in your family?

Working in the Death and Dying Industry over the past seven years, I've come to the realization that if one has not experienced the loss of a loved one and made decisions regarding their final wishes, it is difficult to comprehend how quickly things can spiral out of control if there are no discussion or pre-planning in place. The unpleasant surprises come in the form of chaos, confusion, possible family disputes and family hardships.

If you are anything like me and do not like surprises, I challenge you to ask six to ten friends to share with you their experience of losing a loved one. Ask them what could have made their experience less difficult or if they had any regrets in how things were handled? Hearing about their personal experiences will give useful insights on the importance of having a plan in place before a crisis happens.

Personally, it got to the point where the more heart-breaking stories I heard from different families, the more I realised the depth of the knowledge gap I had on the subject of death. I realised a pressing need to work harder to get information out there to help people understand how important it is to have a plan in place.

I am confident that speaking to your friends who have lost loved ones and have had to make permanent decisions regarding final wishes will reveal how many negative surprises they experienced after losing a loved one. Unsurprisingly, this is because death is a topic many people consider as taboo and, in most cases, families keep it to themselves. If my assumption is wrong, and I hope it is, then it means that more conversations are being had and more families want to ensure that their family experiences would be a positive one for years to come.

Closing

Will your final departure be a smooth or turbulent flight for those who are left behind? The choice of a turbulence free flight is firmly in your hands. A final departure without a clear itinerary in place increases the likelihood of chaos, confusion, family disputes, financial hardships, inability to properly grieve, involvement of external parties (such as government) and the possibility of not having your final wishes carried out accordingly.

The best part about this flight and having a clear itinerary is that you can pack and prepare for the flight way in advance. Choosing whether you are there to personally put the oxygen mask on your loved one's face or guiding them step-by-step through your final destination (of death) is an act of love. This will guarantee a smooth flight and reduce the likelihood of your family having to figure things out on their own. Reviewing and filling out the workbook will allow you to hold your loved ones by their hands and guide them through this part of your final destination.

I hope you have started to have the crucial conversations with your family and have begun the process of getting your affairs in order for your final departure.

Hopefully, this book has provoked you to delve further into understanding the process of preparing for your final departure. This will be a great benefit to both you and your family in providing a welcomed relief in a devastating time and allowing them to freely grieve, knowing that your final wishes are carefully documented in detail for those who remain.

As we all know, the only time we have is now, as tomorrow is not promised. Therefore, it is imperative to take the initiative today, set aside all fears, or taboos to prepare for one of life's inevitable or, as some would say, the unavoidable which is death, before it is too late.

For successful completion of this flight, I ask that you explore the resources shared throughout this book and seek assistance from the experts in your respective city, province/state, and country. A workbook is included with a step-by-step user-friendly guide to assist you with completing varying tasks at each phase of your planning.

At the back of this book, you will find different resources:

- A list of grief and bereavement books for children and adults and other books including senior care.

- Learning how to communicate with a loved one who is critically ill or dying.

- Tips on how to set up a meal train for friends and family who have lost a loved one(s).

- What to say and what not to say when communicating with a griever.

- Information on where to order the death deck game, a lively family game of surprising conversations about death.

- Various End-of-Life Professionals and Vendors primarily in Alberta, Canada.

Most importantly, the workbook at the back of this book will help your family when you are no longer around. The workbook starts with a step-by-step guide on the end-to-end process on what to do in the first 24 hours of a passing, seeking out assistance from professionals and planning the Celebration of Life Service.

These sections will help your loved ones during that devastating time, so, remember to inform them about this book and where it may be in your absence.

What you do today will impact how you are remembered for your Legacy. So, let's put a plan in place today and live the best life.

As my mentor Rhonda Green has said *"Take care of the business of dying.... so you can focus on living."*

"On behalf of Legacy Airlines and the entire crew, I'd like to thank you for joining us on this trip."

IN LOVING MEMORY OF

Folasade (Sade) Abiola

You left such an amazing legacy for so many of us to learn from. I have recently learned that our Legacy is the ultimate person we want to become, and you mastered that far more than many of us could ever imagine. You showed many of us - both young and old - the true meaning of kindness, humility, loyalty, consistency, generosity, selflessness, love and unshaken faith and trust in God.

It is still mind-blowing how you found the time to be so much to so many people. You managed to remember names of everyone including family members you never even met but always asked about, you remembered birthdays, anniversaries and the list goes on. Your consistent encouragement for us praise team leaders and your thorough long text messages to many will be immensely missed along with your various emojis.

On my birthday this year you sent me a long message and part of the message reads: "So my dear Sister Andrea, as we look forward to this year for and with you, I see great, wonderful and marvellous things that God has planned for your life, things to move you forward in the right direction to bring glory and honour to His name continually in your life, making you a shining light in our community in the mighty name of Jesus. Our loving Lord is just starting with you, my dear friend and Sister. Strive for the best, the Lord is on top of the REST 🖤😍☺️."

Oh my goodness, I don't think you knew I was writing this book, but I claimed what you said in Jesus' name. No words can explain how much those words meant to me. The day before you died your last few words to me were: "How was the attendance at the Seminar? I hope people gave it a lot of thought and invited their families and friends. You are doing your best making yourself visible in the community and I know God will continue to bless all your efforts in Jesus' precious name 🖤☺️

Thank you so much, Sister Sade, for being so much to so many of us and for showing us what it means to leave an amazing Legacy that we can strive to work on just with the little things, starting with love. We love you and you will be greatly missed. Rest on, our Queen, until we meet again.

Letter of Instructions to My Loved Ones

If you are reading this letter, it means I am no longer with you, but do not worry, everything is going to be ok. I have all the information that you need to help you during this difficult time in this workbook.

I know that you are in shock, confused, and possibly do not even know what to do. Yes, it's ok to feel anger towards me, after all, I left you.

I wanted to make sure that you have nearly everything you need; this workbook is mostly in the order of what is necessary to get things done. From the moment of my passing to what you will need to help you with almost everything after. There is information on which funeral home to call, my final wishes, where to find all my important paperwork, my celebration of life preferences, and much, much more.

I am sorry I had to go, but please never forget that I love you and please take care of each other. Remember and celebrate the life we shared and all the good times we had together. Focus on all the good things and look to the future even as you mourn my departure.

Live life to the fullest, continue to create amazing memories with each other, create a bucket list and work on completing it.

Tomorrow is not guaranteed but living your best life and loving each other unconditionally will leave no room for regrets.

Hoping to soothe your hurt with lots of love,

Signature _____
Date   _____

What to Do at the Time of Death

When a Death Occurs

At Home: If the deceased was under hospice care, contact the hospice nurse. If not under hospice or palliative care and the death was not expected, call 911.

At a Hospital: The doctor or nurse on duty will ask which funeral home you would like to care for your loved one. Let them know, and also, contact the funeral home of your choice. At the hospital, at times, you do have some time to figure out which funeral home because there is a morgue onsite.

At a Hospice: Let the hospice facility know which funeral home you would like to care for your loved one and contact the funeral home. Please keep in mind that in most cases this decision will need to be made right away because in most cases, there is no morgue onsite.

At a Nursing Home or Long-Term Care Facility: Let the nursing home or long-term care facility know which funeral home you would like to care for your loved one and contact the funeral home. Please keep in mind that in most cases this decision will need to be made right away because in most cases, there is no morgue onsite.

Abroad: Find a funeral home in the region where the death occurred that is experienced in international funeral arrangements. The funeral director will guide you through the next steps and help you with arrangements in both countries if you decide to repatriate the body or cremated remains back home.

Bringing a loved one back home can be very difficult especially when dealing with different languages, laws and cultures.

If Canadian, go to:

https://travel.gc.ca/assistance/emergency-info/death-abroad   or contact the nearest Canadian Embassy or Canadian Consular Services in the country where the death occurred.

If American or from another country, contact your Embassy or Consular Services for your country, in the country where the death occurred.

1-4 Hours After

Contact Immediate Family

- Try to contact all immediate family members first and ask them to assist in helping with calling other family members before contacting other friends.

- Even though news travels fast and every friend has a friend who has a friend, try to ensure immediate family members do not find out from others or on social media.

Contact Religious Leader/s

- If your loved one was a part of a church family or religious group, contact their leader to notify them of the death.

Choose and Contact Funeral Home

- Hopefully, there is a funeral home of choice chosen and your loved one has a pre-arrangement set up or a file started at a funeral home.

- If not, either ask their community/religious leader or close friends for suggestions.

- If you mentally can handle doing research during this time, contact two to three funeral homes from their suggestions and get quotes, remembering to compare apples to apples.

Once a funeral home is chosen, contact the funeral home and questions they might ask you are:

- Full name of your loved one who died?

- Where did they die and where are they currently?

- What is the name and contact details of the next of kin?

- Does your loved one have a pre-arrangement with their funeral home?

- What is your name and contact details if you are not the next of kin?

Contact Other Support Helpers

- Think of a support team to help with the various responsibilities that will be needed during this devastating time. This could be a family member, a close friend or a third party.

- Assign someone to manage incoming calls. Ensure there is always a pen and paper around to take messages.

- Have a team or someone to help with funeral arrangements.

- Have family or a close friend to help with the basic things like errands and children and to be your right-hand person.

Overall, there will be a lot of decisions to be made in a short time depending on how much was done in advance and taking care of yourself during this difficult time will be crucial. This will be emotionally, physically, and mentally draining.

4-12 Hours After

Prepare to start making Celebration of Life plans (Funeral or Memorial Service)

Track down all important documents

- Insurances.

- Funeral Pre-arrangements (Prepaid funeral package).

- Will.

- If no funeral pre-arrangements are in place and if you do not know your loved one's final wishes, ask other family members.

Gather Vital Statistics Information to Bring to the Funeral Home

- This information is what the government collects at the time of death.

- Refer to Workbook for more information (Vital Statistics)

Contact Employers

- Both for the deceased and loved ones who will need time off.

Contact Insurance Agents

- Look for all insurance that would cover a death claim.

12-24 Hours After

Self-Care and Rest

- Try to rest and take care of yourself because it is going to get very busy between organizing things, taking phone calls, visitors, and a lot of emotions. Taking care of your loved one's final arrangements and taking care of yourself requires a lot of energy. Ensure to feed yourself properly. Eating during this time is very difficult so drinking Ensure and supplement drinks will help to keep you going.

Gather Pictures and other Remembrances of Your Loved One

- Check the desktop, laptop or iPad for a folder that says pictures, your loved one might have a folder on their devices.

- Finding pictures and other remembrances to memorialize your loved one at the Celebration of Life gathering will be important and a part of the grieving processes. Setting up a special area at the place of service of special things to remember your loved ones and other items will be personal and meaningful.

Figure Out How The Funeral/Memorial Will Be Paid For

The funeral home and cemetery bill are two separate bills and, in most cases, will need to be taken care of before the service. Getting a clear understanding of where the money is coming from and what the budget is will save you hundreds or thousands of dollars depending on the funeral home. The greater the pain, the deeper some will go into their pocket. Be very careful of emotional overspending during this difficult time. If there is no pre-arrangement set up at the funeral home, below is a list of where possibly you can start looking to know where this money will be coming from, now or at a later date. This way you will have a budget idea.

- Life Insurance Policy (if you can avoid it, do not assign the insurance policy to the funeral home, especially if you do not know the value of it).

If you do not know if there is any insurance set up, check the mail for bank statements showing monthly charges from an insurance company. Keeping in mind that only the beneficiaries can call into the insurance Company.

- Veterans Burial Benefit.
- Work Benefit.
- Bank Account (if there is money in the deceased bank account, in some cases, depending on where you live, the bank will do up a bank draft to the funeral home directly).

If it is very evident that the deceased did not leave any money to take care of the funeral or cemetery bill, you, as the Executor, next of kin or loved one, will need to help to figure out this bill one way or another.

In some cases, families will rally together and figure out the bill, especially, knowing when there is money coming in, and they will be, hopefully, reimbursed. Please, please, please do not allow this bill to cause problems amongst families. This is one of the top reasons for family breakdowns after a passing.

If there is no money coming in and the deceased has no money and you as an Executor, next of kin or loved one is not able to financially take care of the bill, be truthful with the funeral director. And dependant on where you live, there might be some government support that would first be processed through an application to verify that the deceased has no assets or money. Going this route will hopefully manage most of the bill.

Otherwise, options to take care of the bill would be not limited to:

- Cash
- Cheque
- Credit Cards
- Bank Loan
- Go fund Me

Allow Yourself To Grieve

Taking the time to grieve and accept what is happening and letting out your emotions is part of the grief process. Throughout the days, you will just need to cry it out and you will notice how healing it is. Holding it in and trying to be strong will not help you in the long run. It is helpful to be around those who understand and are supportive especially when you are nervous, and your tears seem like they will never stop. Those healthy tears are needed.

WORKBOOK

CERTIFICATE
OF LOVE

This section contains my important information and final wishes

_____
My Name

My accountability partner/partners   **We as accountability partners will work together to get most or all of this workbook completed in:**

Name _____

Name _____

☐ 1-3 months   ☐ 3-6months   ☐ 6-9 months   ☐ 9-12 months

We do understand that the sooner we get this done, the sooner we will have peace of mind knowing that our families will be better prepared with step by step instructions during that devastating time. Once complete, we will live our lives to the fullest because tomorrow is not promised.

Print Name and Sign _____ Date _____

Print Name and Sign _____ Date _____

Print Name and Sign _____ Date _____

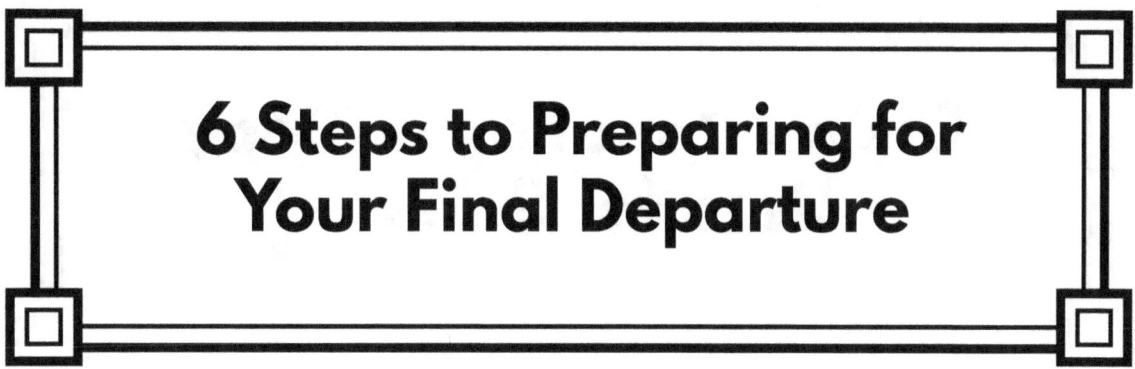

6 Steps to Preparing for Your Final Departure

Date Completed:

Step 1 - Have the Conversation with Your Family

- Senior Care Options
- Do Not Resuscitate (DNR)
- Organ(s) Donation
- Final Disposition Wishes
- Where To Find Important Documents
- What To Do With Your Stuff

Step 2 - Get a Will and Two Living Wills

- Will
- Two Living Wills

Step 3 - Get Insurance

- Term Insurance
- Final Expense Insurance
  (ex. Funeral Home Prepaid Policy)

Step 4 - Research and Choose a Funeral Home and/or Cemetery

- Funeral Home
- Cemetery

Step 5 - Continue Completing Workbook

Step 6 - Live Life to the Fullest

Organ Donation or Body Used for Science

I Want To Donate My Organs: ☐ Yes   ☐ No

I Registered My Request At: _____
Dated: _____
Telephone Number: _____

I Want The Following Organs Donated:

☐ Lung   ☐ Heart   ☐ Kidney   ☐ Pancreas

☐ Cornea   ☐ Bones   ☐ Skin   ☐ Heart Valves

Notes: _____
_____
_____
_____
_____

I Want My Body Used For Science: ☐ Yes   ☐ No

I Registered My Request At: _____
Dated: _____
Telephone Number: _____

Funeral Home & Cemetery Contact Details

Funeral Home Information

Establishment Name _____
Telephone Number _____
Address _____

I Have A File Opened At The Funeral Home?   ☐ Yes   ☐ No

I have A Prepaid Funeral Arrangement Set Up?   ☐ Yes   ☐ No

Notes: _____
_____
_____
_____
_____

Cemetery Information

Establishment Name _____
Telephone Number _____
Address _____

I have a file opened at the cemetery? ☐ Yes ☐ No

I have a plot purchase? ☐ Yes ☐ No

Notes: _____
_____
_____
_____
_____

EMERGENCY CONTACT DETAILS

First person to contact at the time of my death:

Next of Kin
Name _____
Relationship _____
Telephone #1 _____
Telephone #2 _____
Street Address _____
Province/State _____
Postal/Zip Code _____
Country _____

My Executor #1
Name _____
Relationship _____
Telephone #1 _____
Telephone #2 _____
Street Address _____
Province/State _____
Postal/Zip Code _____
Country _____

Family & Friends Contact Details

My Executor #2
Name _____
Relationship _____
Telephone #1 _____
Telephone #2 _____
Street Address _____
Province/State _____
Postal/Zip Code _____
Country _____

Name _____
Relationship _____
Telephone #1 _____
Telephone #2 _____
Street Address _____
Province/State _____
Postal/Zip Code _____
Country _____

Name _____
Relationship _____
Telephone #1 _____
Telephone #2 _____
Street Address _____
Province/State _____
Postal/Zip Code _____
Country _____

Name _____
Relationship _____
Telephone #1 _____
Telephone #2 _____
Street Address _____
Province/State _____
Postal/Zip Code _____
Country _____

Name _____
Relationship _____
Telephone #1 _____
Telephone #2 _____
Street Address _____
Province/State _____
Postal/Zip Code _____
Country _____

Name _____

Relationship _____

Telephone #1 _____

Telephone #2 _____

Street Address _____

Province/State _____

Postal/Zip Code _____

Country _____

Name _____

Relationship _____

Telephone #1 _____

Telephone #2 _____

Street Address _____

Province/State _____

Postal/Zip Code _____

Country _____

Name _____

Relationship _____

Telephone #1 _____

Telephone #2 _____

Street Address _____

Province/State _____

Postal/Zip Code _____

Country _____

Name _____
Relationship _____
Telephone #1 _____
Telephone #2 _____
Street Address _____
Province/State _____
Postal/Zip Code _____
Country _____

Name _____
Relationship _____
Telephone #1 _____
Telephone #2 _____
Street Address _____
Province/State _____
Postal/Zip Code _____
Country _____

Name _____
Relationship _____
Telephone #1 _____
Telephone #2 _____
Street Address _____
Province/State _____
Postal/Zip Code _____
Country _____

Name _____

Relationship _____

Telephone #1 _____

Telephone #2 _____

Street Address _____

Province/State _____

Postal/Zip Code _____

Country _____

Name _____

Relationship _____

Telephone #1 _____

Telephone #2 _____

Street Address _____

Province/State _____

Postal/Zip Code _____

Country _____

Name _____

Relationship _____

Telephone #1 _____

Telephone #2 _____

Street Address _____

Province/State _____

Postal/Zip Code _____

Country _____

Name _____
Relationship _____
Telephone #1 _____
Telephone #2 _____
Street Address _____
Province/State _____
Postal/Zip Code _____
Country _____

Name _____
Relationship _____
Telephone #1 _____
Telephone #2 _____
Street Address _____
Province/State _____
Postal/Zip Code _____
Country _____

Name _____
Relationship _____
Telephone #1 _____
Telephone #2 _____
Street Address _____
Province/State _____
Postal/Zip Code _____
Country _____

Name _____
Relationship _____
Telephone #1 _____
Telephone #2 _____
Street Address _____
Province/State _____
Postal/Zip Code _____
Country _____

Name _____
Relationship _____
Telephone #1 _____
Telephone #2 _____
Street Address _____
Province/State _____
Postal/Zip Code _____
Country _____

Name _____
Relationship _____
Telephone #1 _____
Telephone #2 _____
Street Address _____
Province/State _____
Postal/Zip Code _____
Country _____

Name _____

Relationship _____

Telephone #1 _____

Telephone #2 _____

Street Address _____

Province/State _____

Postal/Zip Code _____

Country _____

Religious Leader/s Contact Details

(Pastors, Priest, Maulana, Pandit, Clergy, Imam, Rabbi, Granthi etc)

Name _____
Church Affiliation _____
Telephone #1 _____
Telephone #2 _____
Street Address _____
Province/State _____
Postal/Zip Code _____
Country _____

Name _____
Church Affiliation _____
Telephone #1 _____
Telephone #2 _____
Street Address _____
Province/State _____
Postal/Zip Code _____
Country _____

Name _____

Church Affiliation _____

Telephone #1 _____

Telephone #2 _____

Street Address _____

Province/State _____

Postal/Zip Code _____

Country _____

Important Documents Log

SAFE DEPOSIT BOX

Location of Box _____
Location of Keys for my Executor _____

PREPAID INSURANCE (Funeral Home Pre-Arrangement)

Pre-Need Policy	☐ Yes	☐ No

Policy or Account # _____
Policy Is Stored _____
Agents Name _____
Telephone # _____
Company Name _____
Telephone # _____
Address _____
City _____
Province/State _____

(Purchased with Pre-paid Funeral Plan)
☐ Worldwide Travel Insurance   ☐ Final Document Service

INSURANCE

Life Insurance Policy ☐ Yes ☐ No
Policy or Account # _____
Policy Is Stored _____
Agents Name _____
Telephone # _____
Company Name _____
Telephone # _____
Address _____
City _____
Province/State _____

Life Insurance Policy ☐ Yes ☐ No
Policy or Account # _____
Policy Is Stored _____
Agents Name _____
Telephone # _____
Company Name _____
Telephone # _____
Address _____
City _____
Province/State _____

Life Insurance Policy ☐ Yes ☐ No
Policy or Account # _____
Policy Is Stored _____
Agents Name _____
Telephone # _____
Company Name _____
Telephone # _____
Address _____
City _____
Province/State _____

Medical Insurance Policy ☐ Yes ☐ No
Policy or Account # _____
Policy Is Stored _____
Agents Name _____
Telephone # _____
Company Name _____
Telephone # _____
Address _____
City _____
Province/State _____

Disability Insurance Policy ☐ Yes ☐ No
Policy or Account # _____
Policy Is Stored _____
Agents Name _____
Telephone # _____
Company Name _____
Telephone # _____
Address _____
City _____
Province/State _____

Auto Insurance Policy ☐ Yes ☐ No
Policy or Account # _____
Policy Is Stored _____
Agents Name _____
Telephone # _____
Company Name _____
Telephone # _____
Address _____
City _____
Province/State _____

Home Insurance Policy	☐ Yes	☐ No

Policy or Account # _____
Policy Is Stored _____
Company Name _____
Telephone # _____
Address _____
City _____
Province/State _____

NOTES: _____
_____
_____
_____
_____

LAWYER/ATTORNEY

Will	☐ Yes	☐ No
Living Wills	☐ Yes	☐ No

Will has been given or stored _____
Living Wills has been given or stored _____
Lawyer/Attorney Name _____
Telephone # _____
Company Name _____
Address _____
City _____
Province/State _____

ACCOUNTANT

Accountant Name _____
Telephone # _____
Address _____
City _____
Province/State _____

Accountant Name _____
Telephone # _____
Address _____
City _____
Province/State _____

FINANCIAL PLANNER

Name _____
Telephone # _____
Company Name _____
Telephone # _____
Address _____
City _____
Province/State _____

BANKING AND ACCOUNTS

Account # _____

☐ Savings   ☐ Checking   ☐ Credit Union

Company Name _____
Telephone # _____
Address _____
City _____
Province/State _____

Account # _____

☐ Savings　　☐ Checking　　☐ Credit Union

Company Name _____
Telephone # _____
Address _____
City _____
Province/State _____

Account # _____

☐ Savings　　☐ Checking　　☐ Credit Union

Company Name _____
Telephone # _____
Address _____
City _____
Province/State _____

CREDIT CARDS/LINES OF CREDIT

Account # _____

☐ Credit Card　　☐ Line of Credit

Company Name _____
Telephone # _____
Address _____
City _____
Province/State _____

Account # _____

☐ **Credit Card**   ☐ **Line of Credit**

Company Name _____
Telephone # _____
Address _____
City _____
Province/State _____

Account # _____

☐ **Credit Card**   ☐ **Line of Credit**

Company Name _____
Telephone # _____
Address _____
City _____
Province/State _____

Account # _____

☐ **Credit Card**   ☐ **Line of Credit**

Company Name _____
Telephone # _____
Address _____
City _____
Province/State _____

Account # _____

☐ **Credit Card**   ☐ **Line of Credit**

Company Name _____
Telephone # _____
Address _____
City _____
Province/State _____

NOTES: _____
_____
_____
_____
_____

REAL ESTATE

Mortgage Account # _____

☐ Joint   ☐ Single

Paperwork is stored _____
Company Name _____
Telephone # _____
Address _____
City _____
Province/State _____

Mortgage Account # _____

☐ Joint   ☐ Single

Paperwork is stored _____
Company Name _____
Telephone # _____
Address _____
City _____
Province/State _____

NOTES: _____
_____
_____
_____
_____

GIC's, BONDS, RRSP & OTHER INVESTMENTS

Policy or Account # _____
Policy Is Stored _____
Company Name _____
Telephone # _____
Address _____
City _____
Province/State _____

Policy or Account # _____
Policy Is Stored _____
Company Name _____
Telephone # _____
Address _____
City _____
Province/State _____

Policy or Account # _____
Policy Is Stored _____
Company Name _____
Telephone # _____
Address _____
City _____
Province/State _____

Policy or Account # _____
Policy Is Stored _____
Company Name _____
Telephone # _____
Address _____
City _____
Province/State _____

Policy or Account #   _____
Policy Is Stored   _____
Company Name   _____
Telephone #   _____
Address   _____
City   _____
Province/State   _____

NOTES: _____
_____
_____
_____
_____

MEDICAL

Doctor's Name   _____
Telephone #   _____
Address   _____
City   _____
Province/State   _____

Doctor's Name   _____
Telephone #   _____
Address   _____
City   _____
Province/State   _____

Doctor's Name _____
Telephone # _____
Address _____
City _____
Province/State _____

Doctor's Name _____
Telephone # _____
Address _____
City _____
Province/State _____

Hardware Login Information

Cell Phone Telephone # _____

Password Given To (Name) _____

Notes: _____
_____
_____
_____
_____

Cell Phone Telephone # _____

Password Given To (Name) _____

Notes: _____
_____
_____
_____
_____

Laptop # _____

Laptop Login _____

Password Given To (Name) _____

Notes: _____
_____
_____
_____
_____

Laptop # _____
Laptop Login _____
Password Given To (Name) _____
Notes: _____
_____
_____
_____
_____

Desktop # _____
Desktop Login: _____
Password Given To (Name) _____
Notes: _____
_____
_____
_____
_____

iPad # _____
iPad Login _____
Password Given To (Name) _____
Notes: _____
_____
_____
_____
_____

Vital Statistics

(Information needed at the funeral home)

First _____
Middle _____
Last (Incl. Maiden Name) _____

Street Address _____
Province/ State _____
Postal Code/Zip Code _____
Country _____

Gender   ☐ Male   ☐ Female   ☐ Non-Binary

Date of Birth _____
Place of Birth _____
Country of Citizenship _____
Live in what City _____
Resided here since _____
Live in what Province/State _____
SIN/ SSA _____
Health Card Number _____

Father's Name _____
Place of Birth _____

Mother's Name _____
Mother's Maiden Name _____
Place of Birth _____

Marital Status Single ☐ Married ☐ Separated ☐ Divorced ☐ Widowed ☐

Date of Marriage _____
Name of Spouse _____
Spouse Maiden Name _____

Occupation _____
Employer/ Industry _____
Date of Employment From: _____ To: _____

Occupation _____
Employer/ Industry _____
Date of Employment From: _____ To: _____

Occupation _____
Employer/ Industry _____
Date of Employment From: _____ To: _____

Veterans/ Military Service

_____
_____
_____
_____
_____
_____
_____
_____
_____
_____

FUNERAL HOME & CEMETERY INSTRUCTIONS

Celebration of Life Service ☐ Yes ☐ No

☐ Traditional with Burial
☐ Traditional with Cremation
☐ Tradional Graveside Service
☐ Memorial Service
☐ Direct Cremation (No Service)

☐ Viewing then Cremation

Visitation ☐ Family Only ☐ Family & Friends

Urn Selection _____

Purchased ☐ Yes ☐ No

Embalming ☐ Yes ☐ No ☐ Unsure

Open Casket ☐ Yes ☐ No
Closed Casket ☐ Yes ☐ No

Casket Selection _____

Purchased ☐ Yes ☐ No

Viewing with:

Glasses	☐ On	☐ Remove
Jewellery	☐ On	☐ Remove

Burial with:

Glasses	☐ On	☐ Give To Family
Jewellery	☐ On	☐ Give To Family

Preferred Clothing
Color _____

New	☐ Yes	☐ No
Out of my Closet	☐ Yes	☐ No

Special Request: _____
_____
_____

CREMATION

I would like my ashes to be:

☐ Given to my family to keep

☐ Earth burial after Cremation
　Location: _____

☐ Columbarium Niche or Crypt
　Location: _____

☐ Scattered by my family
　Location: _____

Special Request: _____
_____
_____

CEMETERY

☐ I Own Cemetery Property
☐ I Do Not Own cemetery property

Final Resting Place

☐ Earth Burial
☐ Mausoleum

Other _____
_____

Name of Cemetery/ Mausoleum _____
Address _____
City _____
Province/State _____
Section _____
Lot _____
Block _____

Vault Selection _____
Purchased   ☐ Yes   ☐ No

Marker or Monument _____
_____

Purchased   ☐ Yes   ☐ No

Company Name _____
Telephone Number _____

If no, inscription instructions

Inscription Details
(Message can usually be around 6 words or depends on cemetery guidelines)

_____
_____
_____
_____
_____

Notes:

_____
_____
_____
_____
_____
_____
_____
_____
_____
_____

ABOUT ME

(Obituary & Eulogy Information)

Spouse _____

Wedding Date _____

Previous Spouse _____
Marriage Dates _____

Previous Spouse _____
Marriage Dates _____

Children
_____
_____
_____
_____
_____
_____

Stepchildren
_____
_____

_____
_____
_____
_____

Parents

_____
_____

Stepparents

_____
_____
_____
_____

Siblings

_____
_____
_____
_____
_____

Stepsiblings

_____
_____
_____
_____

Grandparents

_____

_____

Step Grandparents

_____

_____

Nieces and Nephews

_____

_____

_____

_____

_____

_____

Fiancé

_____

Pets

_____

_____

_____

Others

___

Immediate family who died before me

___

Education

___

Employment Information

___

Military Information

___

Accomplishments

___

Hobbies

___

Favourite Vacations

___

Favourite Foods

___

Some of my fondest memories

_____
_____
_____
_____
_____
_____

Volunteer Positions

_____
_____
_____
_____
_____
_____
_____
_____
_____

A final message for my family and friends to be read at my Celebration of Life

_____
_____
_____
_____
_____
_____
_____

Other Information

_____
_____
_____
_____
_____
_____
_____
_____

Refer also to the Legacy Section in the back of this book

My Eulogy and Obituary

_____
_____
_____
_____
_____
_____
_____
_____
_____
_____
_____
_____

Continued...

CELEBRATION OF LIFE INSTRUCTIONS

Location

☐ Funeral Home   ☐ Church   ☐ Graveside   ☐ Other

Venue Name _____
Telephone Number _____
Address _____
City _____
Province/State _____

Pastor/Clergy
Choice #1
Name _____
Telephone # _____

Choice #2
Name _____
Telephone # _____

Choice # 3
Name _____
Telephone # _____

Funeral Colors
_____
_____

Favourite Flowers
_____
_____

Favourite Scripture Reading
_____
_____
_____
_____

Favourite Poem
_____
_____
_____
_____

Favourite Quotes
_____
_____
_____
_____

Favourite Hymns/Musical Selections

_____
_____
_____
_____
_____
_____

Soloist/Choir Name(s)

_____
_____
_____
_____
_____

Tributes (Who I would like to do a tribute)

#1
Name: _____
Relationship: _____
Telephone Number: _____

#2
Name: _____
Relationship: _____
Telephone Number: _____

#3
Name: _____
Relationship: _____
Telephone Number: _____

#4
Name: _____
Relationship: _____
Telephone Number: _____

Participants Names (Those whom I would love to be apart of my service)

_____
_____
_____
_____

Continued...

_____
_____
_____
_____
_____
_____

Pallbearers

1. _____
2. _____
3. _____
4. _____
5. _____
6. _____

Back Up Pallbearers

1. _____
2. _____

Honorary Pall Bearers

1. _____
2. _____
3. _____
4. _____

Special Request

_____
_____
_____
_____
_____

Reception/Repast Location

_____
_____
_____
_____

Notes:

_____
_____
_____
_____
_____
_____
_____
_____
_____
_____
_____

Examples of Celebration of Life Order

Example #1

- Musical Prelude
- Processional
- Welcome/Acknowledgements
- Opening Hymn
- Opening Prayer
- Scripture Reading
- Musical Selection
- Tribute#1
- Tribute#2
- Tribute#3
- Reflection of a Father/Mother
- Musical Selection
- Poem
- Eulogy/Obituary Reading
- Video Tribute
- Musical Selection
- Sermonette
- Prayer of Comfort
- Closing Hymn
- Closing Prayer
- Recessional
- Burial
- Reception/Repast

Example #2

- Musical Prelude
- Processional
- Welcome/Acknowledgements
- Musical Selection
- Tribute#1
- Tribute#2
- Tribute#3
- Reflection of a Father/Mother
- Musical Selection
- Poem or Favorite Quotes
- Eulogy/Obituary Reading
- Video Tribute
- Musical Selection
- Recessional
- Reception/Repast

Letters for My Loved Ones

Letter # 1

Name: _____

Letter # 2

Name: _____

Letter # 3

Name: _____

Letter # 4

Name: _____

Letter # 5

Name: _____

My Legacy

(What I do today will impact how I will be remembered for my legacy)

How do I want to be remembered?

1. _____
2. _____
3. _____
4. _____
5. _____

What accomplishments do I want to leave for my Legacy?

1. _____
2. _____
3. _____
4. _____
5. _____

Who do I want to impact or help and why?

1. _____
2. _____
3. _____
4. _____
5. _____

These are some family traditions that we have that I would love it to continue for generations to come.

1. _____
2. _____
3. _____
4. _____
5. _____
6. _____
7. _____
8. _____
9. _____
10. _____
11. _____
12. _____
13. _____
14. _____
15. _____
16. _____
17. _____
18. _____
19. _____
20. _____
21. _____
22. _____
23. _____
24. _____
25. _____

My Bucket List

(Things I want to do before I kick the bucket)

Date Completed:

1. _____   _____

2. _____   _____

3. _____   _____

4. _____   _____

5. _____   _____

6. _____   _____

7. _____   _____

8. _____   _____

19.

20.

21.

22.

23.

24.

25.

26.

27.

28.

29.

30.

31.

32.

33.

34.

35.

36.

37.

38.

What To Do with My Stuff

(Keep for my Family)

What To Do with My Stuff

(For Donation)

What To Do with My Stuff

(Notes)

Notes

Grief and Bereavement Books

Children Books

Healing a Child's Grieving Heart
(100 Practical Ideas for Families, Friends and Caregivers)
Alan D. Wolfelt. PH.D.

The Memory Box
(A Book About Grief)
Joanna Rowland

Water Bugs and Dragonflies Explaining Death to Children
Doris Stickney

Till We Meet Again
(A Children's Book About Death and Grieving)
Julie Muller and Camryn Cox

Adult Books

It's Ok That You're Not Ok
(Meeting Grief and Loss in a Culture That Doesn't Understand)
Megan Devine

The Grief Recovery Handbook
John W. James and Russell Friedman

Finding Meaning
(The Sixth Stage of Grief)
David Kessler

Grief One Day at a Time
(365 Meditations to Help You Heal After Loss)
Alan D. Wolfelt Ph.D

The Hot Young Widows Club
(Lessons on Survival from the Front Lines of Grief)
Nora McInerny

You Can Heal Your Heart
(Finding Peace After a Breakup, Divorce or Death)
Louise L. Hay and David Kessler

Senior Care Books

We Can Do This!
(Adult Children and Ageing Parents Planning for Success)
Lorraine Lorrie Morales

Live Life Fully
(30 Days of Easy Projects so that the Rest of your Life is Fabulous)
Jill Burk

Death Preparation Books

My Exit Plan
(Getting My House In Order)
Rhonda D. Green

Talking About Death Won't Kill You
(The Essential Guide to End-of-Life Conversations)
Dr Kathy Kortes-Miller

Family Game

The Death Deck
(A Lively Game of Surprising Conversations) (Ages 13+)

To order, go to:

Canada: https://ddnbc.com/membership-%26-shop/ols/products/the-death-deck

USA: www.thedeathdeck.com

Meal Train

Meal Train simplifies the organisation of meal giving around significant life events like the passing away of a loved one. They strive to simplify and promote interpersonal relationships between friends, families, and neighbours through meals.

For more information, go to: **www.Mealtrain.com**

Things to Say to a Dying Person

- I'm proud of you for _____
- Thank you for _____
- I will remember you when _____
- You are special to me because _____
- Something I want you to know is _____
- I will always remember the time when _____
- You are the light of my life, you bring me joy when _____
- I will never forget you, you _____
- I am so grateful that you taught me the importance of _____
- I love you.
- It is going to be ok (let them know everything is going to be ok even when you know it is not, this is to comfort them).
- I will continue to pray for you.
- You mean so much to those around you.
- I forgive you.
- I just want to let you know that I am thinking of you.
- You are a light in my/our life.

- I know it may be a scary time for you, whenever you are afraid, just know we love you, we are thinking of you and praying for you.
- Our love for you will live forever.
- You are in my heart and dreams forever.

What to Say and What Not to Say to a Griever

What to Say

- I am so sorry for your loss.

- I wish I had the right words, just know that I care.

- I don't know how you feel, but I am here to help in any way I can.

- You and your loved one will be in my thoughts and prayers.

- My favourite memory of your loved one is…

- I am always just a phone call away.

- We all need help at times like this, I am here for you.

- I am usually up early or late if you need anything.

- Just calling to let you know I am thinking about you.

- Always use the language the griever is saying (e.g., dead, gone, passed away).

What Not To Say

- At least he/she lived a long life, many people die young.

- She/he is in a better place.

- He/she brought this on himself/herself.

- There is a reason for everything.

- Aren't you over her/him yet, she/he has been dead for awhile now?

- You can have another child.

- He/She was such a good person God wanted him/her to be with him.

- I know how you feel.

- He/She did what he/she came here to do, and it was his/her time to go.

- Be strong.

At times, it is better not to say anything and just be with your person or just give a hug.

Also, be specific with your person as to what can you do for them:

- How can I support you?

- I am going to the grocery store, what can I pick up for you?

- I will be by tomorrow to help with e.g., dishes, laundry, grocery shopping, cutting the lawn, shovel the snow etc.)

- What grocery store cards or food take out gift cards can I get you?

- We are here to go to the grocery store for you, what do you need?

Just want to give a personal shout-out and thank you to Heidi Dunstan, a Certified Grief Educator with Leaning Into Grief who has enlightened me with this topic on what to and not to say to grievers. Heidi's husband passed away suddenly and her passion is educating people on what to say and what not to say because of her experience. She believes that as a society we are not taught how to support those who are grieving, or in total, how to grieve when a loved one passes away.

About the Author

Andrea Cox is a Canadian author born and raised in Calgary, Alberta, Canada. She is the founder of Cox Compassionate Planning Services (Preplan First), a company founded in 2021 to help families and communities fully organize their affairs and coordinate Celebrations of Life with loved ones at the time of a passing. She wrote this book in hopes that families would consider putting a plan in place today and then living their best lives, knowing that tomorrow is not guaranteed.

For over four years, Andrea has been working with Getting Your Affairs In Order setting up pre-paid funeral and memorial packages in Alberta and BC. Her passion is educating and helping people normalize discussions around the topic of death through seminars/webinars and various social media platforms. With almost seven years of experience helping families, she looks forward to expanding her reach virtually and to assist more individuals and communities (1-2-1 and/or through upcoming workshops) as an Accountability Coach to help develop plans before a death occurs in the family. For more information, go to www.preplanfirst.com.

During her spare time, Andrea enjoys watching praise and worship videos and being a super auntie to her nieces and nephews.

Bibliography

On-line Citings

Sergio Ortega, 1998, airodyssey.net, accessed 28 December 2021,
https://airodyssey.net/reference/inflight/

Dignity Memorials, accessed 30 December 2021,
https://www.dignityfunerals.co.uk/what-to-do-when-someone-dies/when-someone-dies-abroad/

Grief.com, accessed 30 December 2021,
https://grief.com/10-best-worst-things-to-say-to-someone-in-grief/

A Place For Mom, accessed 30 December 2021,
https://www.aplaceformom.com/caregiver-resources/articles/comfort-the-dying

Legacy Project, accessed 15 December 2021
https://www.legacyproject.org/guides/whatislegacy.html

Growth Tactics, accessed 20 January 2022
https://www.growthtactics.net/leave-a-legacy-what-is-a-legacy/

Government of Canada, accessed Feb 7, 2022
https://travel.gc.ca/assistance/emergency-info/death-abroad

Book Citing

Rhonda D. Green, My Exit Plan Workbook, Rhonda D. Green, 2019

WILLS, ESTATES & NOTARY

MARRAZZO LAW OFFICE

1. Do you have your LAST WILL AND TESTAMENT?

A Will allows you to choose who will get *your assets*, who will look after *your children*, and who will be in charge of distributing *your estate*.

Dying without a Will may cost your family and friends hardship, money, and confusion.

2. Do you have your LIVING WILLS?

These documents allow you to appoint someone to make your decisions in the event you become mentally incapable, better known as ENDURING POWER OF ATTORNEY (for financial decisions) and PERSONAL DIRECTIVE (for healthcare decisions).

3. How much is this going to cost me?

BASIC TESTAMENTARY PACKAGE (3 documents)
- This includes your basic WILL, ENDURING POWER OF ATTORNEY, and PERSONAL DIRECTIVE.
Call today for a quote.

4. When can I meet with the Lawyer?

Call today to schedule your appointment.
Same day appointments subject to availability. Evenings and weekends available.
Mobile appointments available (selectively) *extra fee (ex: small towns, hospitals, senior homes, residences)

Call us today at (780) 756-5500

9535 - 135 Avenue   Edmonton, AB.   T5E 1N8

(Northgate Professional/Medical Centre - small brick building across from the mall - FREE PARKING)

GRIFFITHS INSURANCE & FINANCIAL SERVICES
Building strength from root to continuous fruit

Glen and his team work with individuals, families and businesses in Alberta and several other Provinces

At GIFS, we help families, individuals and businesses protect themselves and control the flow of cash. We do that so they can maximize opportunities during their lifetime while controlling and building their Legacies for generations.

Griffiths Insurance & Financial Services
100, 6001 1A St SW, Calgary, AB, T2H 0G5

Email: glen@g-i-f-s.ca
Website: www.g-i-f-s.ca

Phone: 403-273-7200 and
1-855-GAP-GIFS (1-855-427-4437)

Resolve Psychotherapy & Consulting Inc

Mercy Maviko, MSW, RSW, RCSW
Resolve Psychotherapy & Consulting Inc.

Phone: (587) 432-5491
Website: resolvetherapy.ca

Mercy is a Clinical Social Worker who works alongside people struggling with:

- Trauma / PTSD
- Depression
- Eating disorders
- Guilt and Shame
- Anxiety, panic attacks and phobia
- Loss and grief
- Low self esteem
- Emotional dysregulation - e.g. anger and irritability
- Emotional Neglect
- Relationships (romantic, social, and occupational)

PIERSON'S
FUNERAL SERVICE LTD.

Honouring and remembering every life

Your full service funeral home specializing in
Church and Graveside Services · Preplanning
Burial · Cremation · International Shipping

*Dedicated to **quality** funeral service at **affordable** prices*

A Family Owned and Operated Business
serving Calgary and Area since 1983

4121 – 17 Avenue SE, Calgary, Alberta T2A 0T1
403-235-3602 (24 hours)   **www.piersons.ca**

CSD MEDIA

We'll help you tell your story!

Specializing in photo and video storytelling for over 15 years

WWW.CSD.MEDIA

CUNNINGHAM LAW
PROFESSIONAL CORPORATION
BARRISTERS, SOLICITORS & NOTARIES

EXPERIENCED • TRUSTED • RESULTS

Family Law

- Divorce/Annulments
- Custody/Access
- Child/Spousal Support
- Support Termination
- Prenuptial Agreements
- Separation Agreements
- Property Division
- Restraining Orders

Wills & Estates

- Wills/Codicils
- Powers of Attorney
- Probate
- Estate Administration
- Estate Litigation
- Guardianship Applications

and Other Matters...

Free initial 1/2 hr consultation
Evening, Weekend, & Virtual Appointments Available
Special Discount to HRPA Members, Family and Friends

Karen Cunningham, Senior Counsel
Hons (B.A.), Juris Doctor (LL.B.)
Over 23 years legal experience

Email: lawyers@cunninghamlawpc.com
www.cunninghamlawpc.com
T: 905-270-8075

Toronto, ON

SELL MY STUFF CANADA
Need To Sell Your Stuff?

Canada's largest and most respected high-end content and estate sale company

- *Full service – we run content and estate sales from your home*
- *No cost to you – we operate based on an agreed-upon percentage of the income from the sale as our fee*
- *One - stop solution for downsizing, de-cluttering, moving or estates*
- *Professional, stress-free experience*
- *Access to a large customer base*

Servicing Alberta, Ontario and Quebec
Call MARCY today at 1-855-55-STUFF

Email: calgary@sellmystuffcanada.com
Website: www.sellmystuffcanada.com

INTERNATIONAL DOULA LIFE MOVEMENT invites you!

CALLED TO BE A DOULA

END-OF-LIFE CERTIFICATION • CONTINUING EDUCATION • INSTRUCTOR SUPPORT • BUSINESS BUILDING • SECURE ONLINE COMMUNITY • RESOURCES • AND MORE!

INTERNATIONALDOULALIFEMOVEMENT.COM

Trinity Funeral Home
www.trinityfuneralhome.ca

Edmonton Family Owned Funeral Home

780.474.4663

"everything a funeral home should be..."

NEW HAVEN FUNERAL CENTRE INC.

Ask me about creating your Legacy...Your way

7025 Legion Rd., Mississauga, ON L4T 1A8
(Just minutes from the airport)

Minnelle Williams
Pre-Planning Funeral Director

Phone: 647.640.8922 | 1.833.363.9428
Email: preneed@newhavenfc.ca
Website: www.newhavenfuneralcentre.com

MJB PSYCHOLOGICAL SERVICES LTD

During these difficult times, MJB Psychological Services Ltd. offers online grief and bereavement counselling in Alberta and Ontario to those who have lost a loved one.

Michelle J Buckle
Registered Psychologist & Dramatherapist

Phone: (780) 757-8255 (TALK)
Website: www.michellejbuckle.ca

SHAUNA DAVÉ

Specializes in Wills and Estates

Shauna Davé
BA. (Hons), LL.B, LL.M.
Barrister, Solicitor & Notary Public

Phone: (403) 870-0276
Fax: (403) 265-0573
Email: shaunadavelaw@gmail.com

Tower Centre West
#438, 131 - 9 Avenue S.W.
Calgary, Alberta T2P 1K1

JUDICIOUS HOME CARE SERVICES

Promoting Quality of Life
Through Personalized Services

Services We Offer:

- Senior Care
- Respite Care
- Companionship
- Non-Senior Care
- 24/7 Personal Care
- Special Needs Care
- End of Life Care
- Homemaking Services
- Medication Reminders
- Post-Surgical Non-Medical Care
- Alzheimer's, Dementia and Parkinson Care

Hilda A. Ngeche
Care Manager

Phone: (403) 397-3846
Email: info@Judicioushomecareservices.com
Website: judicioushomecareservices.com

FINANCIAL CONCIERGE

We work with seniors and their families around Estate documents and administration.

Jill Chambers
BN CFP CEA

Phone: (403) 978-2176
Website: www.financial-concierge.ca

Need a Basic Will? Executor?
Enduring Power of Attorney?
Agent for Personal Directive?

Call us! We can help

MEMORIAL GLASS KEEPSAKES
An experience. A memory. A gift.

The loss of a loved one is difficult and Glass House is here to help you through the process. Using less than a teaspoon of cremated remains our team of trained glass artist will handcraft a keepsake of your choice in your color scheme. The final product is something you can cherish and hold for a lifetime. Order online and follow mailing directions. **We ship worldwide!**

Phone: (403) 462-2651
Email: info@ghxperience.com
Website: www.ghxperience.com

Cherish
photo preservation & scanning

Preserving Your Family Legacy

With over 30 years of working in the creative industry, I'm an avid photographer and photo enthusiast. I am passionate about photos and the precious memories they hold. They are unique to each and every person and they are priceless!

Convert your photos, negatives, slides & children's artwork into digital images. Create a family album, slide show of an event or just have them preserved and archived.

Digitizing all your photos protects your memories from floods, fire, fading, or getting lost or damaged.

Services
Photo Scanning of prints, negatives & slides.
Custom Family Albums
Slideshows *(Memorial - Special Occassion)*
Photo Restoration
Digital photo management/consulting.

For more information & pricing call or email
403.615.4575
email: cherishphotos@shaw.ca
www.cherishphotos.ca

Servicing Alberta & Canada wide.

LET TOMORROW BEGIN TODAY...
Plan ahead for Peace Of Mind.

Pre-Planning
Customized Service Packages for Local Funeral Homes

Estate Documentation
Aftercare Document Preparation

World Travel Protection
Costs and details protection if death occurs while travelling

Emergency Kit
FREE gift with purchase for all your important documents

FREE Estate Planning Seminars/Webinars
Join Pre-Planning experts and get answers here

If someone had to make sense of your financial matters without your help, would they know what you owned, where you kept your will and insurance policies, or even who you wanted to take care of your pet? Think about it...

NOW may be the time to get your affairs in order.

WE CAN HELP!
1-866-250-1825

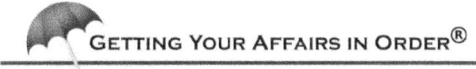

Areas we currently serve in Canada:

Alberta

- Calgary and Surrounding Area
- Edmonton and Surrounding Area

Yukon Territories

- Whitehorse, YT

British Columbia

- Armstrong, BC
- Castlegar, BC
- Kamloops, BC
- Kelowna, BC
- Lake Country, BC
- Nakusp, BC
- Penticton, BC
- Thompson, BC
- Trail, BC
- Greater Vancouver & Fraser Valley, BC
- Vernon, BC
- Victoria, BC

IN ORDER TO KEEP YOU TICKING, WE NEED TO KNOW **WHAT MAKES YOU TICK?**

PLAN WELL

Serious illness, like a heart attack or major traffic accident, can occur to any of us at any time. When you are seriously ill, you may be unable to communicate –but there are decisions that have to be made about your care. In these situations, doctors will usually turn to your family who will have a very difficult time and will experience significant stress if they haven't discussed your wishes and values beforehand. We know that these topics can be difficult to discuss –but they are important.

To optimally prepare for the future, please do the following:

1 See your lawyer and fill out official paper work to designate someone to be your appointed decision maker if you're unable.

2 With your decision maker, visit the url: *planwellguide.com*, a new medical planning tool, and review the information, make your plan, and print off a copy of the "Dear Doctor" letter (the output of the plan). Share a copy of this letter with your appointed decision maker. form.

3 Keep these important medical care planning documents with your other important documents and have them present when you go to hospital.

CONGRATULATIONS!

You are on your way to preparing for the future! Your family will thank you.

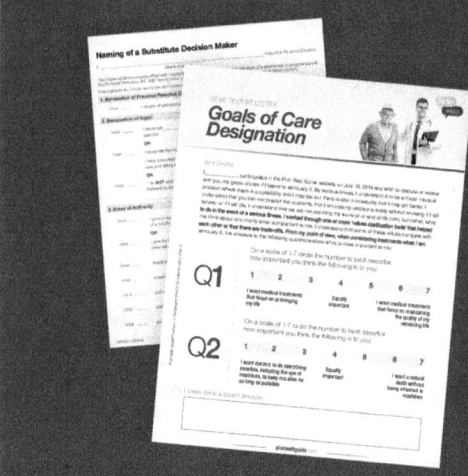

I HAVE A PLAN

Make a plan at *planwellguide.com*

Pierson's Funeral Service Ltd.

Family run since 1983

Website: www.piersons.ca

Locations

Calgary

4121 17 Ave SE
Calgary, AB, T2A 0T1

Phone: (403) 235-3602
E-mail: info@piersons.ca

Cochrane

#6–Sundance Mall
402 Railway Street West
Cochrane, AB, T4C 2B6

Phone: (403) 932-1039
Email: cochrane@piersons.ca

Flower Gallery

4121 17 Ave SE
Calgary, AB, T2A 0T1

Phone: (403) 248-2400
E-mail: info@piersons.ca

Everden Rust Funeral Services & Crematorium

Family run since 1970's

www.everdenrust.com

Locations

Kelowna

1910 Windsor Road
Kelowna, BC, V1Y 4R5
Telephone: 250-860-6440

Kelowna West

190, 2300 Carrington Road
West Kelowna, BC, V4T 2N6
Telephone: 250-768-8925

Penticton

1130 Carmi Avenue
Penticton, BC, V2A 3H2
Telephone: 250-493-4112

Trinity Funeral Home Ltd.

Family Owned Funeral Home

10530-116 S, Edmonton, AB, T5H 3L7
Telephone: 780-474-4663

www.trinityfuneralhome.ca

New Haven Funeral Centre Inc.

Specializing in Meaningful Funerals,
Funeral Estate Preplanning & Worldwide Shipping

7025 Legion Rd., Mississauga, ON, L4T 1A8
(Just minutes from the airport)

Telephone: 905.678.8922
Toll Free: 1.833.363.9428

E-mail: info@newhavenfc.ca
Website: www.newhavenfuneralcentre.com

osujismith.ca (403) 283-8018

41 YEARS OF EXCELLENCE

SPECIALIZE IN

WILLS AND ESTATES

EMPLOYMENT LAW, BUSINESS LAW, DIVORCE & FAMILY LAW, CIVIL LITIGATION LAW, REAL ESTATE LAW

www.ingramcontent.com/pod-product-compliance
Lightning Source LLC
Chambersburg PA
CBHW081707100526
44590CB00022B/3688